/ICE

D1627518

A SHROPSHIRE
BOYHOOD

A SHROPSHIRE BOYHOOD

PETER DAVIES

FOREWORD BY
JULIAN PETTIFER

ISIS
LARGE PRINT
Oxford

Copyright © Peter Davies, 2006

First published in Great Britain 2006
by
Sutton Publishing Limited

Published in Large Print 2007 by ISIS Publishing Ltd.,
7 Centremead, Osney Mead, Oxford OX2 0ES
by arrangement with
Sutton Publishing Limited

British Library Cataloguing in Publication Data
Davies, Peter, 1928–
    A Shropshire boyhood. – Large print ed.
    (Isis reminiscence series)
    1. Davies, Peter 1928– – Childhood and youth.
    2. Country life – England – Shropshire – History –
    20th century
    3. Large type books
    4. Shropshire (England) – Biography
    I. Title
    942.4'5'084'092

ISBN 978–0–7531–9436–2 (hb)
ISBN 978–0–7531–9437–9 (pb)

Printed and bound in Great Britain by
T. J. International Ltd., Padstow, Cornwall

To my family and friends,
past and present,
who shaped and shared with me
this goodly heritage

It was the best of times, it was the worst of times,
it was the age of wisdom, it was the age of
foolishness,
it was the season of Light, it was the season of
Darkness,
it was the spring of Hope, it was the winter of
Despair,
we had everything before us, we had nothing
before us,
we were all going to Heaven, we were all going
direct the other way.

Charles Dickens, *A Tale of Two Cities*

Contents

Foreword

Peter Davies must be my senior by a few years, but, judging from his book, he spent most of his childhood in Shropshire during the third and fourth decades of the last century, just as I was growing up in Wiltshire. For those of us of a certain age who were raised in English villages, this book is an excellent evocation of time and place and of the spirit of an era. It is also warm, funny and acutely observed.

Younger readers who have borrowed my copy of the book were enchanted by it but also slightly incredulous. Could the ablutions and the sanitary arrangements have been quite as primitive? Yes, they could. Were rural communities really that isolated and self-sufficient? Yes, they were.

Just as I did, Peter Davies went rabbiting and bird's-nesting and grew up with the legends and casualties of the First World War. On every page I find there is something that strikes a chord. When Davies writes about his father's Welsh pony, Dorothy May, and how she frequently brought his father home safely when he was incapable with drink, I was instantly reminded of my grandmother's black pony. He was called Nigger (no pony could be so called today), and Nigger frequently found his way back from Devizes market with the driver sleeping in the trap.

Peter Davies's description of the Shropshire village school brings back such painful and vivid memories of my own Wiltshire C. of E. primary that I can almost feel my smarting knuckles and smell that distinctive odour of chalk and grubby children.

Peter Davies is a poet, and his prose writing demonstrates that he has a remarkable ear. He has a wonderful description of hunting rabbits with sticks and terriers: "the binder . . . had reduced the standing crop to that fateful triangle from which the hopeless rabbits had to run." It took me back sixty years and I relived the excitement of it all.

Then there is Peter Davies the dramatist! Apart from the boyhood adventures and the antics of his siblings and schoolmates, there is a cast of adults observed by the clear-eyed and unsentimental boy. It is worth reading *A Shropshire Boyhood* just for the account of Jimmy Roberts and "Jimmy's fiery mum, with a head like a thornbush and eyes like live coals [who] used to sing like a versatile nanny-goat, always cooking, always singing in her comfortable, carefree, cavernous house."

Alas, my own boyhood did not yield a Jimmy Roberts or his mum, but thanks to Peter Davies, I can share the joy of them. This is a little gem, difficult not to collect and to treasure.

Julian Pettifer

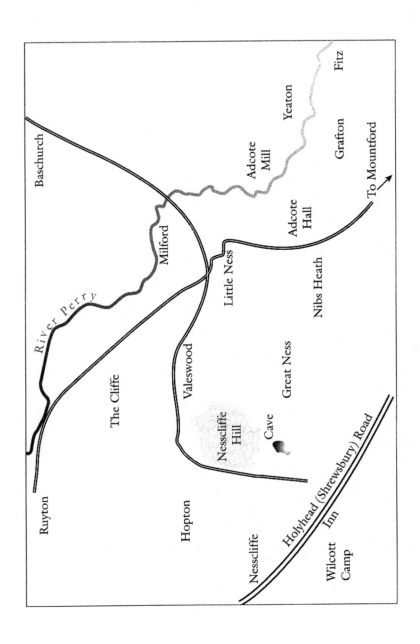

CHAPTER
ONE

Our Village

Ninety-nine miles to Holyhead, a hundred and sixty-two to London, said the brilliant yellow AA sign that hung like a sun on the wall of our neighbour's roadside barn. But we never went to London and we never went to Holyhead. We lived in the heart of the country in the little-known county of Shropshire, in a village called Little Ness. There stood the school, on a hill; and there was the church; and there, on yet another hill, was the post office, which in 1939 still had its Woodbines, winegums, blotting pads and stamps. There, as a boy of eleven, I stood with my penny sticking to my hand. I looked at the regimental screw-top jars — black and scarlet, gold and blue — embraced as I was and puzzled by the smells, wine-warm and plum-puddingy: the scents of pear drops mixed with ink; of sugared almonds, sealing wax; of glacier mints and sherbet fountains; liquorice allsorts, Bluebird toffees, chocolate cream bars made by Frys; aniseed and nougat and cigarettes and frying fish . . .

"A pennyworth of winegums, please."

The weight went on, the balance swayed, then stopped. And Mrs Garry, knowing that I still had my penny clenched in my hot hand, prised it from me with the offer of "one for luck". I needed the luck.

I stepped outside. There, facing me, was the Red House Farm. It was my father's old home; my uncle's now. It wore a warm red sandstone smile. Its setting was finer than that of the Home Farm, the next largest farm in the village. It was more lustrous than Lower House, though that was where the barn shone with the sign. And our place, Church House, still looked what it was, a disused malthouse. These holdings, and much more, had once been the estate of Alfred E. Darby, Squire, one of the iron-masters of Coalbrookdale. In days gone by they were part of the manor of Oswestry and Clun, owned in succession by the families of de Montgomery, FitzAlan, Howard, Craven, Herbert and Clive.

From 1893 my grandfather, John Davies, farmed 360 acres of prime riverside land, part of the Darby estate; fields with names like Chapel Meadow, The Leasowes, Flaxyards and Clover Piece, which, sloping eastward to a bend in the Perry stream, on sunny days exhale a pride of place and provenance. They were the jewels in the Darby crown. I liked to wander from the post office down Church Lane and through those shining fields.

A pennyworth of winegums went a long way in the spring. They would last me till I reached World's End or the sandy-bottomed hollows of the Cliffe.

The Cliffe is the hill that rises to the north-west of Little Ness, between Ruyton-XI-Towns and Valeswood. Between Valeswood and Nesscliffe stands Nesscliffe Hill, the Cliffe's more noted grown-up brother, part of the Earl of Bradford's fine estate. The Cliffe, on the other hand, is a common with little or no pretence to afforestation. It had, when I was a boy, an open quarry, invitingly exposed. It bred wild tracts of heather, bracken, gorse. It was my playground. It was also the haunt of rabbits, owls, jackdaws and gypsies. To stand on the Cliffe is to experience instant rejuvenation, a rolling back of the years, a sense of paradise regained. Astonishingly, on a clear day, I can see from this pivotal point the three places where I spent my early life. They are all in a direct line: Wigwig, near Much Wenlock; Wigmarsh, near Oswestry; and Little Ness, midway between the two, the centre of our attention in this book.

What else can be seen from the top of the Cliffe? You can, of course, see Ruyton-XI-Towns and Baschurch where my Aunt Mary, Uncle Percy and Cousin Margery lived. You cannot see Nesscliffe because it is tucked away behind the hill, but you can see the towering poplars that conceal Great Ness. Beyond them runs the A5 road, Watling Street, that linked us to Shrewsbury and — supposedly — to London and to Holyhead. You can see as far as the borders of Wales where the Severn loops the foothills of the Breiddens and Admiral Rodney is said to have sighted from Liverpool those oaks which probably provided timber for his ships. A column of stone called Rodney's Pillar points from the top of the Breiddens like a finger testing the wind or feeling the warmth of the sunset's glow. You can see the Callow, a mount shaped like a toadstool, crested with trees, next to the long-tailed Stiperstones. You can see the Long Mynd and Caer Caradoc, the great Church Stretton hills.

I lived among these hills and breathed the legends that they bred. I cannot share them, or my winegums, without recourse to history and some unvarnished facts. But much of my story has, I hope, the flavouring of summer fruits: of raspberries, strawberries, limes . . . and some original, imaginative piquancy.

Beyond the riverside fields, characteristically dotted with good-sized oaks and grazed by clean, sun-dappled dairy cows, our village rises through the trees: a gable here, a group of chimneys there. And shining, almost pealing through a belt of yews, there peers the belfry of our little Norman sandstone church, standing proudly on an earthwork. Here, but you would never know it, a sixth-century Celtic prince died gloriously and was buried in a mound; and there, a well-fletched arrow's flight beyond, a sixteenth-century highwayman carved for himself a niche in legend, if not in academic history.

Little Ness Church is, indeed, the outstanding feature of the village. Its exterior is neat and beautifully proportioned. Its interior is something to behold. It was originally a chapel of ease and was not licensed for baptisms and funerals. People had to go to Baschurch to begin and end their Christian pilgrimage. Once, the shepherds of those quiet pastures and still waters stood in a flock outside their church to demonstrate their anger at the parson from Baschurch, who had long neglected them. He, knowing they were there, appeared; then wilfully and scornfully passed by.

We had no such problems in our day. In the early part of the twentieth century Squire Darby acquired the chapelry of Little Ness and — so wrote our parson in a book — "The Vicar of Baschurch with the consent of the Lord Bishop of Lichfield surrendered to Mr Darby and his heirs and assigns the whole right of patronage, nomination, presentation and appointment to the Church of St Martin. The new patron then gave a site for a parsonage and a suitable house was erected by him at his own expense . . .". Hence our splendid parsonage, which, shrub-ringed, is not quite clear from the Cliffe. Mrs Darby, not to be outdone, added the school, more elevated, plain to see. Our village was munificently endowed.

Then the Great War came and knocked a hole in everything. The Darbys lost their only son Maurice. A lieutenant in the Grenadier Guards, he was killed in action at Neuve Chapelle in 1915. The regimental drum and the young officer's sword were brought back with his body from the battlefield by his uncle, Sir George Arthur. I used to go into the church and peer at the drum reposing on the ledge of a stained-glass window depicting three warrior saints: St George, St Michael and St Maurice. "In glorious hope of the Resurrection and in loving memory of Maurice Darby who died in battle for his country March 11th, 1915, this window is dedicated by his parents Alfred and Frederica Darby" was the inscription that I read.

What, I ask myself, did the Darbys not give to the church? They gave the rood, the reredos, the organ — which I sometimes played; they gave the sanctuary lamp, the lectern, altar hangings and vestments, chairs and other furnishings. And, almost poignantly, as they died, their survivors dedicated to them ever more splendid memorials.

After 1915 the sorrowing squire retreated to his residence at Adcote Hall, built of warm red sandstone from the quarry at Red House. There members of the Royal Family were entertained. Queen Mary herself visited in 1921. But in the year of my story, it was a residential school for girls. The squire had died. There was only the frail and spindly Frederica left. Almost totally deaf, this shadow of a former, more harmonious age encouraged me to raise my platinum voice above the others in the choir. Her loneliness was emphasized by the vastness of Little Ness House where she lived on with her companion, Miss Dowty, in increasingly reclusive style. Another lady, Miss Want, still exercised a string of snuffling, pop-eyed Pekinese about the village. But the staff had dwindled to a chauffeur, a retired coachman, a footman or two and a few pale, whispering maids. We boys still touched our caps to Mrs Darby if we met, as we did to the teacher and the vicar, of course. But the squire had gone, and with him the *raison d'être* of the system. The heart had gone out of the village. There was not much left. Only legends. And a sense that there was a time before our time.

THE DARBYS

The influence of the Darbys was still felt at Little Ness. There was at home a photograph of the young men who left the parish to serve in the Great War. About twenty of them, some in uniform, some not, were grouped outside one of the fine mullion windows of Adcote Hall. Seated though they were, each had, held in his hand, or hooked over an arm, a silver-handled walking stick: a ceremonial presentation, perhaps. Certainly the smart lad in civvies — not sporting his stick — in the back row was my father, though he had been wounded in one arm and one leg. Next to him was Archie Davies from Adcote Mill.

The photograph showed the flower of Little Ness manhood: confident, handsome, proud. I don't suppose one of those lads minded being herded at the Hall, presented with a rather superior-looking cane and photographed like that. (Nobody smiled for photos in those days: it was a rather serious business.) Most of them riding off on their yeomanry horses — but soon drafted into the infantry — thought, no doubt, that the war would soon be over; that each one had the power in his own limbs to "finish it off".

Mrs Darby would still have made a fuss of Dad, if he had let her, instead, it seemed, she made a fussof me. I could sing, loud and high enough for her to hear me in the church choir. She sometimes gave me things. She

7

called me Tom — which was, indeed, my first name. She would call on Mother, using the front door — only used in our experience by Mother rushing out on a Sunday to catch Wagg's bus, and by the parson on a Tuesday afternoon when he wanted a cup of tea. "It's a birthday!" she would bawl, deaf as a post. Their conversation over, Mother would show Mrs Darby out. "You'd better take her a piece of your birthday cake." And, the Sunday after that, I would take back a message from Mrs Darby saying it was delicious.

"Are you sure she didn't say deloshous, or delovely?" Mother was always making up words.

Into that sitting-room at Church House, one afternoon at a cold time of the year, stepped Archie Davies. He had a large, droopy moustache, a heavy fur coat reaching down to or beyond his very high boots, a big wide-brimmed hat and a heavy accent to go with that heavy moustache. He seemed stern. We boys felt of no account in his eyes, but Dad understood him and Mother settled all problems with a cup of tea. John and I went upstairs, leaving them to discuss what sounded like "business". There John could escape into *White Fang* or *Tarzan of the Apes*; I could admire myself in the mirror with the tie (Scottish tartan) that Mrs Mrs Darby had given me for some reason; pretend to be pleased to see my uncle from across the sea; try to find out from John where Canada was ("It's a big place!"); think how much more handsome Dad was when he smartened himself up — but I knew there was a shadow lying over Little Ness and Church House in particular that I could not quite pin down. Only our father — and Uncle Archie, perhaps —

really knew the Darbys when they owned all Little Ness. Once it had been all one big estate, every farm a chick under one broody hen. Mrs Darby still clucked, but the chicks had been left to get on with it, "scratching and scraping for a living" was the phrase.

Warm, it must have been, clutched all together under one leader, the Squire. But he died, suddenly, we were told. Anyway, there was only Mrs Darby left: Frederica Darby, as she signed herself on the church notices. She leaned on the arm of her companion who saw her to her lonely seat by the organ where she sat shrugged in astrakhan and drenched in scent, fiddling with pins with cut-glassheads for the notices, sorting out the numbers of the hymns, the psalms and their chants, the Caleb Simper Eucharist: Kyrie, Agnus Dei . . .

"Thou that takest away the sins of the world," we sang, over and over again. There were only two or of us in the choir now — and not many more in the congregation, sometimes. Dad never came. Mumcame to evensong, late. Mrs Darby shuffled down late. Mrs Darby shuffled down the aisle with her ear trumpet to hear the sermon, then shuffled back to her seat by the organ for the last hymn. The parson usually closed the service with my favourite prayer: "O Lord, support is all the day long, until the shadows lengthen and the evening comes, and the busy world is hushed, and the fever of life is over, and our work is done . . ."

"Shadows of the evening," we sang. Lambs called; rooks called; you could hear them above the thin singing in the church. Maurice Darby's regimental drum was grey with cobwebs on the north-east window ledge. Outside

— if it was spring — daffodils on his grave by the porch stood to attention as if to salute the sun going down in the west; if it was later in the year, the shadows lengthened just the same.

Agriculture and industry had exploded into prosperity in Victorian times, but even before the turn of the century, just as my grandfather acquired his riverside lands, farming was beginning to feel the draught of American competition. The Bromleys and the Davieses had prospered as farmers and corn merchants, and when Adeline Bromley married my grandfather John, it was common for a farmer to have a dozen children. So also was it for farmworkers, who might have had to live on ten shillings a week. And in those days the triple fears of the workhouse, the asylum and the grave haunted all. Even I as a little boy, much later, had heard my father say we should all end up in a workhouse. Shelton Asylum (clearly visible from the Cliffe) was a byword in our society and, alas, through its propinquity drew victims like a magnet. Babies were born and died like chickens. And blood poisoning or pneumonia could just as suddenly claim a man of proven constitution.

My grandparents brought up twelve children at Red House Farm. Six boys, six girls. At home we had a treasured photograph of my Aunt Lottie's wedding. She was my father's eldest sister. I could read that picture like a book. The women all wore enormous veiled hats, each one a wedding-cake caprice. There sat my grandmother, classically poised, a little lace on her collar and cuffs to lighten the generally heavy effect of the late Edwardian style of dress. The men, in jackets not too tightly buttoned up, looked more relaxed, but did not smile. The boys on benches at the back stood to attention, taller than the rest, their necks stretched by their Eton collars, unfamiliar ties and the antics of the photographer disappearing under a black cloth. They were handsome and grave and totally unconcerned about their looks. Grandfather, the founder of this dynasty, had more than a trace of the old Adam in his eyes. He was small and not without a look of pride, and some amusement perhaps, that from so spare a rib as his should come forth so many Eves. Lottie, her veil drawn back, though very beautiful showed no emotion in her face. Emotion, as it turned out, would not have eased the ups and downs of married life that lay ahead.

In the days before the Great War my father's family and the Birchalls, who lived next door at Lower House, would hold great parties in their respective rambling old farmhouses, which set the maids running along stairways and passages, crying "Murder!" in the night. The main rooms were lit maybe with oil lamps, but the corridors would be dim for Sardines, Murder and Postman's Knock. I could imagine the cellars and hay lofts and the pantries in between, crowded with every lusty lad in love with every other wanton wench.

And on Sundays they would all put on Eton collars and Norfolk jackets, long dresses and blousey hats to go and sing soprano, alto, tenor and bass in the choir at

11

church. Mrs Cope-Darby was the choirmaster then. She was a regular martinet, Dad said. Nobody played Murder with her.

I try to picture my father Thomas — still tall, still handsome — as he must have been a generation back. What was he like when all the world was young?

He had always known our house, so near his boyhood home. He knew our two great conker trees — the source of sticky buds in spring — one of which had leaves with five parts, the other leaves with seven; one had smooth and mottled conker shells, the other spiky and green. They smelt of iodine and split white-eyed when ready on the ground, and gave us clean, unhurried sport for days, weeks, months — perhaps a year.

He knew the elm but lately struck by lightning near the church. He knew the oak tree by the school, the Douglas fir that stood, plumed sentinel, on the orchard's edge. He knew the dark and hollow churchyard yews, one large enough to hold the sexton's tools. He knew the enigmatic mound, the earthwork by the church. He knew the endless litanies of Lent.

He knew the gates: the one that led to the orchard and the one that led to the church; and, in between, the little stackyard gate, the easiest way to the walnut tree. He stained his fingers with the walnut juice and passed it off as nicotine. He whittled sticks with a penknife till his fingers ached and thumbs were sore. He peeled the skins off hazel wands in long, long slippery straps of green that left the flashy white flesh cold and sticky underneath.

He knew the lanes: those lanes that lead to nowhere — or everywhere when you are young. He went rabbiting and bird's-nesting and was whacked by the squire. Whenever the squire saw a boy he gave him a whacking. He took the view that if he wasn't getting into mischief then he must be coming from it.

THE RED HOUSE AND THE LITTLE NESS CHURCH

Many of the houses and farm buildings in Little Ness had been built out of stone from the quarry at the back of Red House. It was a lovely red sandstone common to the area; dark, with a touch of romance. Generations of pierced hearts and initials had been carved in it; generations of children played in the quarry, sailing down worn chutes on rusty pieces of tin. Baths, kettles, cups, tea pots, enamel buckets and bowls, pram wheels and the bones of animals found their last resting places there. We wondered whether as children we could have become rich from the treasures we found half-buried in its vasty deeps. It was from this treasure of earth that Red House itself must have been built: the house that, to our eyes, was more outstandingly beautiful, more luminous and, like the quarry, more intriguing, than anywhere else in Little Ness.

We all looked up to the Red House. We would all have liked to have lived there. It was the most prominent house in the village. Even more than the church, it was well set up. A sort of crown: the symbol of a smaller kingdom within a larger one. Oh, yes, and we were bounded by the Shropshire and Welsh border hills; so there were kingdoms beyond, but Red House was enough for us.

It was at the top of the road that ran through Little Ness, from the Ruyton and Valeswood roads in the west, to the Adcote and Baschurch roads in the north and east. The parsonage and school stood between us and the gypsies on the wasteland of the Cliffe, on the one hand, while Little Ness House and Adcote Hall added lustre to our riverside domain, on the other. The Red House stood at the centre of the village, opposite the Post Office and the war memorial, where three roads met. You could not miss it. Red sandstone buildings ranged behind and beside it, but the house presented itself, front of stage, to be applauded and admired. The parsonage was surrounded by shrubs; Little Ness House sat in a small prairie of lawns; Adcote Hall was almost unapproachable for trees — cedars and Wellingtonias. The Red House faced up to the world. Our world. The world that was as near to Eden as you could get.

Just down World's End Lane was the church where we received our earliest — and most lasting — ideas about life. Nobody went to the church that didn't pass the Red House — unless they cut up through our fields at Church House, muck-spread in winter and spring, and rootled by pigs in summer and autumn. The Red House produced more church-wardens than ever Church House did. We were next to Lower House (non-conformists); not total outcasts, but sinners in need of all the uplift we could get.

14

There was no doubt where the saints came from: they were all the well-dressed, well-to-do people residing nearer Adcote, Milford and Baschurch, where, to our eyes, the sun never set. Somehow, it never occurred to us to wonder why they attended church more often than those who lived in less-favoured parts of the village. Our father said that, in the old days, he and they were dragooned there by the Squire. Asked why he did not go to church now, he said he had had enough when he was young. Our mother still felt the need of a slice of evensong: usually the latter half. For children, however, church attendance — choir practice and Sunday school included — was obligatory. It was a kind of medicine, given in prescribed doses; no use feeling ill, it made you better; it sometimes even had an agreeable taste.

Somehow, I could never dissociate the smell of church from the smell of those cedars at Adcote and Little Ness House. We did not have incense; but we were rather High. It is time to consider the influence of those Darbys again. There was a time when Little Ness church was only a chapel of ease to Baschurch. There was a time when, according to Mr Parrott, the leader of the Celts, Prince Kyndylan, was slain here by the invading West Saxons and buried in our mound. He quoted an old Welsh Marwnad or lament:

Bassa's Churches! There rests tonight there ends —
  there shrinks within himself
he that was the Shelter in battle, Heart of the men of
  Argoet!

15

To our young eyes this was sadder than Gray's "Elegy" itself. True, the mound, situated just beside the church, was shrinking within itself and appeared to contain nothing but a few rabbits which we were intent on ferreting out; but the Mound — perhaps more than God's house, perhaps more than the Red House — was invested with magic and mystery. What if Kyndylan — Cynddylan if he really was Welsh — had never existed? There was nothing to prove it; neither was there anything to prove that all those slain in battle in the Bible had existed. We had a mound, which was tangible evidence of some extraordinary event in the past. We were working on it — and if any further evidence came to light we would work on that. A great deal had to be taken on trust; a great deal could be left to the imagination.

My father must have been just like me. He went to the same church, he went to the same school — too often and too long, he claimed. Believe it we did when he told us that Miss Heavens, our old infants' mistress, was a pupil teacher at the same school, shaping pothooks on a slate, when he, a boy of eleven, sat looking up at a new east window, wondering how he could shorten the shadows cast by long division. I sat by that same big window, wondering the very same thing, in 1939.

But at eleven my father already had ideas of leaving school. Sitting under the same schoolma'am from the age of eight till he was fourteen was a prospect no more appealing to him than it was, some thirty years later, to me. He saw his chance when a bucket of water, carried all the way from the malthouse pump, was left in the girls' cloakroom one day, and he was given a message to take to the infants' teacher through that area, normally out of bounds. He made water in the bucket and someone in a pinafore and pigtails saw him. A complaint, a consultation with the managers and Thomas was expelled. He was horsewhipped by his father and made to walk to Baschurch school, three miles away. This was the first great legend of my childhood.

The second great legend, only dimly apprehended by me, was the Great War.

This legend is represented in the portrait of my father as a young lad in the yeomanry. We knew our father must have been a strapping youth, too often strapped for doing wrong, but never so happy as when he was taking a team of horses with corn to Baschurch station and bringing back a load of coal. We knew that he was good with horses, patient and persevering — able to calm them with his touch, and very quick to anger if someone hurt a defenceless beast. We knew that when he was sixteen he joined the yeomanry and that when the war broke out he, so at one with a horse, added a year to his age and rode off like a centaur on the wind.

When my grandfather saw his sons, Tom and Jack, set off in August 1914 to serve their country, little did he know that he would not see them again. It was corn harvest time and something went wrong with the binder. Granddad crawled under the canvas to repair it, got dirt in a boil on his neck and blood poisoning set in. In a matter of days he was dead.

My father came back five years later, broken in body and mind. He, who had known Little Ness so well, had to find a home elsewhere.

Brother John's Stories

Occasionally John would leave the adventures of *The Invisible Man* and tell me one of his own stories, setting poachers above gamekeepers, gypsies above landowners, weaklings above bullies, sinners above saints and — as in the "Magnificat" — exalting the humble and meek. Who else was there to do it? Not Mrs Darby!

John was especially good on Uncle Dick who threw the loaf across the dinner table at Red House and, in a moment of madness, gave away his share of the farm. It was almost biblical in its ferocity and far-reaching effect. What, we wondered, would have happened, if Granddad had had two wives — "and two concubines," added John — and twelve sons instead of only six?

"And if he had lived to be old, like Jacob?"

"And his days had been long in the land which the Lord God gaveth him?"

"And there had been no war?" Sometimes John told the story in a lofty tone: "and Dick departed," as if he were Lot or Abraham. Sometimes he went straight in with no tut-tuts by the girls that were left straightening their backs at the table, smoothing down their pinafores and wondering how they were going to get the milking done. (Dick was the fastest milker on the farm; Tom was still in the army; John, who had gone with him to the war was shell-shocked in the asylum; and Harry was useless since a barn door fell on his head — or so we were told. Billy was too young to milk thirty cows; and Frank, the next in age, was left holding the loaf.)

"So Dick set off, sprinting on his short, fat legs, down the Cow Lane, over the Holyhead road, through the army training grounds, over the Severn, nonstop to Wood End, where he was courting Elsie, the cheerful cheesemaker from Cheshire. On the way, he helped calve one of her father's cows and was given it and Osmarston, the farm next door."

"Steady on!" I said. "What about the dog he left behind at Red House?"

"It kept them awake with its barking all night, so they loosed it and it swam across the Severn and joined its master in the morning."

"How many miles was that?"

"Ten — as the crow flies."

"And Dick didn't take any clothes?"

"Only what he stood up in. It was summer. Fields whitening to harvest. Dick's bin harvesting ever since."

"And never been back?"

"No, never bin back."

It was a marvellous story, much embroidered since — but all the better for being kept short. Like the one about

19

Billy, who in his turn went, too; but he went north, much the same distance — and more harvesting.

Of our mother's childhood and youth we knew less. She gave us in her by-the-way fashion only ill-fitting glimpses of her background, one of which was that her red-headed grandmother had once broken a plate on her head. And that her grandfather, Liverpool's chief librarian, had lived in the same house as the red-headed plate smasher for twenty more or less silent years.

She was an only child; her mother died when she, our mother May, was born. Her father was a doctor living in Hampstead. But he never practised. Only the organ, she said. Bookish and unconventionally educated, Mother had holidayed in France, spoke the language, painted in water colours, and thought of Liverpool and London as her first and second homes.

She had only one blood relative left alive: our Great Aunt Alice. It was this elderly figure of spinsterly rectitude, who actually wore pince-nez and fumbled with her reticule, who chaperoned my mother's youth. But, prudent and shadowy as she was, she showed a proper sense of what a town girl needed when, just before 1914, she brought her niece to stay at Nesscliffe Hotel. They helped decorate the tree at Christmas; and came back in April to pick primroses and walk on the hill. From yearly happy visits the young May Cowell became the friend of Miss Nellie Thonger, the hotel licensee, and, through Miss Thonger, the friend of Miss

Nellie Humphrys, who worked at the hotel when she was not riding pillion on Mr Charlie Birchall's Velocette. Then, one summer eve at the end of the war, young May clapped eyes on a tall, good-looking bombardier. It was the end of Liverpool and the beginning of me.

Mother sent her aunt a telegram one day to say she had been married that morning, and speedily rode off down the Holyhead road to the Isle of Man on the back of Tom Davies's motor-bike.

Then came the struggle. My father's first venture in farming was at Wigwig, near Much Wenlock, launched by Mother's capital. It did not prosper. The farm was stocked with choice milch cows, but money could not make them hold their calves. Contagious abortion stalked the steep-sloped fields and Mother was sickened at the sight of cleansings floating down the gurgling brook. My father turned to pigs. There would be no milking. There would be plenty of swill and whey from the creamery. Pigs were not fussy. But foot-and-mouth struck. The market was frozen. The pigs could not be moved.

In the years that followed at Wigwig the family fortunes did not improve, so finally we exchanged the steep, unlucky slopes of Wenlock Edge for the weeping wetlands of the Wigmarsh, near West Felton, Oswestry. Born in Wenlock, I was laid in a clothes basket with my twin sister Laura and, conveyed by pony and trap with our elder brother John, we were rumbled across the country on a north-westerly axis to the Wigmarsh, where, I imagine, our mother rested the basket in the reeds. She stayed there only long enough for another child, my little sister Belle, to be born before deciding on a lodging in the middle ground, a little higher and much dearer to her heart.

So, in 1929, we came to Little Ness. There was a good crop of hay. Enough to keep five cows. Pigs were down. Try hens. Egg money came in regularly, like the milk cheque . . . But to ride the terrible storms that in the years of depression sucked down many a bigger ship, a smallholder would have had to be sober and attentive at all times to his craft. It was only by careful husbanding (if that is the word) of what she called her own bit of money that Mother was able to keep our little ship afloat. Needless to say, it was she, the Captain, who also swabbed the decks.

Through all her tribulations Mother put on a brave face. She still went to the Grand National every year. She used to run, splay-footed, very early on a Saturday morning, all the way to Baschurch, catch a train to Chester, connect for Liverpool, and report to us at midnight who had won. The greatest excitement was in 1936, I think, when Davy Jones's reins broke and Reynoldstown won the second time. She never put any money on him but we cherished his picture on a cigarette card that fell from one of the many packets of twenty Players that she smoked.

A little later in the lightening year she would go to that other National dear to her heart: the National Gallery in Trafalgar Square. It was typical of Mother that she said she only went to London to renew her acquaintance with the Duchess of Milan.

Christina of Denmark, Duchess of Milan, was only sixteen when Holbein painted her, in mourning for her first husband. Under that black head-dress and sable furlined gown, the little cuffs and ruff of lace, there beats the heart of youth. And the eyes and hands of Christina are indeed as tenderly expressive of loss as Paul Cezanne's *La Vieille au chapelet*.

Religion was a help to Mother too. Though nearly always late for services, she liked to have the church nearby. She believed, she said, in bulwarks. In the sitting-room cupboard full of her grandfather's books she kept her mother's Bible and her Book of Common Prayer. Alongside books by Mrs Henry Wood and books in French like *Figures et choses qui passaient* was one which her grandfather had written about the library.

Mother loved her books, as she loved the music hall, the cinema and the travel of the mind. Even as she was scrubbing the kitchen tiles she listened to the matinée on the wireless; as she darned sock after holey sock of an evening, she was transported by "The Man in Black". There she would sit, withdrawn, her mind only partly engaged by the work in hand, the firelight playing on her cheek. It was not only her finely tuned temperament that set our mother apart. She had the looks that might have belonged to a great actress: the face oval and aquiline; the dark hair parted high, almost in the middle and drawn back lower over one eye than the other, with a terrace of curls over each ear.

She was a marvellous conjuring cook. After muck spreading we would come home to a rousing stew with suet dumplings, followed by thick yawning slices of golden apple pie.

She was also endlessly resourceful. "Needs must," she'd say or "*Je m'en fiche!*" as she tried to get a sulky fire to draw. "Ah, *courant d'air!*" Then she'd bang the door, and all the smoke would go outside. She'd grasp an iron, spit on it, and press the clothes so hard the veins protested in her arm.

It was Mother's special gift to be able to turn darkness into light, to defy the doldrums and the blues, the dullness and the dinginess, the dangers even that beset our lives. Her spit and polish, elbow grease and gumption were the physical extension of a superior mental resilience. Mother had mettle.

And she had competence. Whatever order there was in our lives was introduced by her. Regular meals and regular medicine. Splash went the eucalyptus for our colds; ditto the iodine on our cuts. To see her swing a bandage, you knew she'd been a VAD.

She would steal up at night and give our chests a rub with camphorated oil while we were sound asleep. And in the morning dose us with our California syrup of figs, our fruit salts and liver salts — Eno's and Andrew's — fighting us out of the glass. She dug in our ears with a handkerchief, cut our nails too near the quick and threatened to choke us when she sewed top buttons on our shirt. "Why is it always the top one that goes!" She wound the cotton round and round and snapped it with her teeth. I swung my head back just in time for a dose of brimstone and treacle to be thrust into my mouth "to do your liver good!"

"We'm never bad!" John would holler as he pulled me off my feet with the crosscut saw. He meant we were never ill. We lived out of doors. The large, three-storeyed house of slate and stone, cellared, shuttered, damp, draughty and cold, was mostly for feeding and sleeping in. Hams and flitches of bacon hung there, while yet more hams and flitches lay in vinegar and saltpetre on slabs of slate in a larder where the temperature would cure anything. There was a fire in the kitchen, a black-leaded grate, my father's rail-backed chair, the settle (we called it the "screen"), the long deal table with benches on either side, a slop stone, a boiler, a mangle and a cupboard under the stairs.

Occasionally, in the evenings, after my father had left in search of his nightly drink, we would retire to the sitting-room, where the fire and the Aladdin lamp transformed the scene. John, his hands over his ears and both elbows on the table, might be far away with Captain Cook; Laura deep in the *Swiss Family Robinson*, screwing up her concentration by twisting with her forefinger one favoured lock of hair; and Belle the Little Mermaid herself, sitting with feet tucked firmly away for safety under her skirt. Mother would be sewing and trying to listen to the wireless while I made a nuisance of myself, getting between her and the light. Over our sitting-room fireplace was a blank wall, whitewashed or distempered perhaps, a perfect theatre for shadow play. Here with practised hand I would bring to life the Indian, the wolf, the long-eared owl.

We "played" in the loft over the kitchen sometimes, too, but there was more fun in working outside. Water had to be carried from the pump in the little yard. (We washed under its cold, invigorating spout and spat at the geese when we brushed our teeth, and they spat back at us.) On the two sides of the little yard were the vast two-storeyed barns with winches, trap doors, stairs and dark, unfathomable holes. Where you could see you could not safely tread for treacherous floorboards lay ahead, as like or not to let you down. We had written our names in pencil years before, on clouds of cracked old cow-hair plaster hanging loose. I was christened Thomas Peter, but always called by my second name. When I was six I thought Peter Thomas was my name, and P.T. my initials. It was a long time before I got them round the other, right and proper way.

The little yard was big enough to enclose the pump, two or three chicken coops, bantam runs, a pig boiler, a coal hole, two pear trees, a damson tree and Caroline.

Caroline was where you went after breakfast to make sure you would be all right for the day. You went again before dusk to make sure you would be all right for the night. She (Caroline) was whitewashed, scented with Jeyes and very confidential. You knew if someone was coming down the path by the crunch of cinders underfoot. We never locked the lavatory or any other door. Torn squares of *Home Notes* gave you all the help you needed if your boy had gone off with another girl. What you did if it was the other way round you never found out. It did not give advice to boys whose girls had served them with that trick.

Beyond the little yard lay the big yard with its cobbled causeway, shippons and stable on one side, pigsties and stackyards on the other. And everywhere the tidal, whalebacked "mixen" of manure. We spent our lives defying its encroaching blue-black, bulked-with-straw embodiment of stench.

There was a right of way through our big yard and the fields that led to the church; but few were the timid churchgoers who'd tread that path when we were spreading muck. We couldn't have been much closer to the church and its companion mound, those timeless bulwarks in our lives. They exercised a strange, almost mystical beneficence on us.

When I look at our little holding today, I see it just as it was when I was a boy. There is the white fold gate. Next to it is a stone on which my father often sat, his cap tilted back and his cigarette burnt to an inch of ash, telling his tales of the war. He had been badly wounded at Wipers (as he called Ypres) and, in a world of summonses and bills, of policemen, vets, magistrates and banks, consoled himself with alcohol.

"No more than the rum ration we had, sir, when we went over the top!" That was what he was reported to have told the magistrate when Sir Offley suggested that my father just might have had too much to drink.

He had a pony, I can see her now, black Dorothy May, grazing on the top field there with our little grey Welsh mountain mare, Topsy, tossing their heads together, companionably, at rest. The black pony was a legend around Nesscliffe and Little Ness. She was that rare thing, a great, good-hearted driving mare — and blessed with second sight. Many's the time she brought my father home without error on a dark night when he was incapable with drink. She skipped past dangers like a swallow. She skimmed the edges of night and slipped through shadows like a bat.

"I 'eard yo father goin' 'ome last night," I remember the blacksmith at Nesscliffe saying. "I'd know that pony anywhere! And 'er'd lost a shoe!" I tried to change the subject but it's hard to get a blacksmith to follow another line of thought. Hammer, hammer . . . "'Old up, yer so and so!" He hit the pony on the rump with the wood of his hammer. Thump! But Topsy only leant on him, making the air blue with smoke from the hot iron meeting her hoof and making his language worse. "It was after twelve o'clock. 'Er was goin' a good lick — no lights, I don't suppose. A livin' legend is that mare. 'Er's got six senses, second sight and magic shoes! Up with 'er 'eels and away like the wind!"

I could imagine him lying in bed listening to the rapped tattoo. "'Er's lost a shoe! And Tommy's 'ad too much of Thonger's brew! *Tu-whit, tu-whoo!*"

Though stuck in "the back of beyond" Mother always kept in touch with her friends. The wind-blown Wirral "aunts" drove up in open tourers with tulled hats. They set down hampers full of clothes before our disbelieving eyes. They wore navy blue and white and passed on school blazers and cricket flannels which had never been near a damson tree, barbed wire or cow-dung-spattered grass. They bore away fresh eggs, dressed chickens and fruits according to the season.

Two more of Mother's friends, who had all the glamour and spontaneity of fairy godmothers, were Auntie Nellie Birchall, Nellie Humphrys that was, and our teenage cousin Margery. Auntie Nellie was "proper Welsh". She worked at Nesscliffe Hotel but she was born, we were told, near Pistyll Rhaeadr (Llanrhaeadr), one of the wonders of Wales — where shepherds washed their flocks, said John. He had been there, seen the waterfall with the rainbow in the spray, and stayed with Auntie Nellie's nephew Eddie who, at thirteen, could already shear the sheep and run, lift, drive, fetch, gather, shed and pen them with his dog: those sheep that looked most like the white and chubby long-tailed lambs we saw in the stained-glass windows in our church.

For a long time I thought that babies came from the waterfall. Was it because, as John said, it dropped from heavens high? I thought they landed in a kind of pump stone, cushioned with moss like the one in our farmyard. I had heard so much about the famous waterfall and read about it in George Borrow's *Wild Wales*. It was somewhere over the hills and far away.

Auntie Nellie would come by bus to Great Ness turn and walk by Ness Strange, through the Poplars Field, down the old Cow Lane. Small and neat and trim, she usually wore a suit of blue or pink; a matching, sunny hat; a cameo brooch and pearls. "You look as if you've just stepped out of a band box," my mother always said. For a woman who worked so hard, my aunt was indeed miraculously spruce. She washed her face in buttermilk. She had apple-blossom cheeks. But, small and white-haired as she was, she reminded me of the wild white cherry: clean and fresh and just as tough.

She often took my sisters Belle and Laura home with her, to get them out of the way, and give them lessons in cooking and decorating and seeing to the visitors. Spring cleaning was a kind of sacrament to her: an outward and visible sign of an inward and spiritual grace. I never saw anybody invest work with so much fun. And the girls came away laughing and ready for more — which was indeed her well-considered aim.

My teenage cousin Margery was no relation to Auntie Nellie but shared with her those gifts which are so precious to children: laughter and still listening. She too came from a place of enchantment: Baschurch Corner Stores. Margery was beautiful, dark and mischievous. To my delight she tickled me unmercifully. Oh, I was very touchable and tender about the ribs! All the way down three flights of stairs I would roll, sometimes in paroxysms of delight and pain. But I couldn't stop laughing and that was my undoing. Shirt-tail out, giddy, flushed and sore, I was ordered to practise the piano while Margery was invited to titivate my mother's and my sisters' hair. She wrought a transformation on the girls. She tweaked their locks with curling tongs, twirled dextrously above a saffron flame. I shut out the evil smell of the methylated spirit lamp and thumped out Chopin's *Polonaise* ("The Military") on the Collard & Collard in the Empty Room. I had heard Solomon play it on the wireless and — like Mussorgsky's *Gopak* — I had tackled it untutored and alone.

After all the repeats had been repeated and octaves doubled in the bass I gained an auditor. Quietly, Margery would slip on to the stool beside me and lower her head. "Play 'Jesu Joy'," she'd say. I knew that off by heart. "Now *Humoreske*." Margery knew how much it meant to me that someone showed they cared.

And when my mother came in looking like the twenties girl in her favourite portrait, I knew why Margery was loved by her. She gave my mother back something she had nearly lost at Little Ness.

Belle and Laura, prinked and preened, always pretended not to know the time. "Get off to bed, you two!" our mother would yell. They took their candles with their cue. Laura was ten minutes older than I. She never let me forget it. Belle, the prettiest, was the youngest by fifteen months. With our primitive washing facilities, going to bed in order of age would have been far too impracticable; and anyway, as they never failed to remind us, girls always go first.

In and out of bed, I had a close, fighting and wrestling relationship with my brother John.

"Say you surrender," he hot-breathed in my ear as I lay on my back and he pinned my biceps down with his knees.

"You surrender," I responded faithfully.

John had won a scholarship and went to the Priory School in Shrewsbury. I was still at the elementary school in Little Ness. He had homework: French, Latin and something called algebra, which, he said, was like arithmetic, only easier. I envied him his greater height,

31

his fairer, curlier hair which crowned a brainier cranium; but he alarmed himself more than me when, still only twelve and at a loss to find a way to press both ears back with the pillow, he remarked that he was going bald.

I felt sorry for John's ears: ears which stuck out so far that in daylight the sun shone through them and showed up the veins. The rest of his head was as hard as an old conker, but his ears came in for a terrible battering. Mother could not resist them. She clouted them at table if he picked up a pea before being told to begin. I would sit in safety by the wall and grin. He would fire a pea at me with his finger and get another clout. "What's that for?"

"To go with the other one" would come the unanswerable reply. But he didn't get bullied, for all that his ears stuck out. Only by Mother.

One night in April 1939, my mother halted me on my way up to bed. She had noticed my shirt cuffs were wet. "Don't you roll your cuffs up when you wash?" she asked.

"Or take your shirt off altogether, like I do," said John, who was always baring his tin ribs at the pump outside.

"As I do," Mother corrected him. "Leave it at the bottom of the stairs and I'll dry it by the fire," she went on. "Good night, boys."

John and I slept in a long, low, tunnel-like room at the back of the house. We were often sent to bed early. Out of the way. Mother probably didn't realise how good for us this was. We read in bed. Anything between covers, you might say. With a flashlight under the sheets. After the stub of candle had gone out. And we talked. We talked about our legends that, like the spiders in our bedroom, came out of the sandstone; they came out of the angles of the ceiling which, on either side, sloped down to low, dark-shadowed walls. They came out of John's head.

I was eager to tell John about my battle in the playground that day with Big Fat Jelly Rump, the biggest bully at Little Ness school. Big Fat Jelly Rump had sandy nostrils and yellow teeth — just like a Tamworth pig. And piggy eyes.

"What's wrong with calling Griffiths Big Fat Jelly Rump? You do," I said to John.

"I'm older than you. I can look after myself."

"I called him Drippin' Tin as well. He bit me on the behind." I pulled up my nightshirt to display the weal of blue indented with the marks of Big Fat Jelly Rump's teeth.

"Fool," said my brother.

"Hell fire," said I.

"Why?" said he.

"Mr Parrott said so. 'He that calls his brother a fool is in danger of hell fire'."

The Reverend P.A. Parrott, our vicar, was the ultimate authority. Detached, pink-skinned and sinless, he passed through our lives — as he walked through the village — clean-shod and clean-shaven; the cleanest living thing on our unclean bit of earth.

"Get into bed, you two!" Mother called from twenty stairs above. "I won't tell you again."

Once in bed we resumed our nightly ritual: summing people up, making up names for them — and reputations.

"Ladies of Little Ness!" John suggested grandly.

"Miss Heavens, the infants' teacher!" I responded, rising to the occasion.

"She rides her umbrella, one hand on her bike, till she alights crosslegged on the kerb by the school."

"She is nimble with drill: arms stretch, feet astride; touch your toes — with a whack of the ruler and a 'Keep your knees straight!' She has a blackboard of pothooks and Ss and tables of fire."

There was another "Shut up!" from Mother, and a "*Taisez-vous donk!*"

After a decent interval we went on to talk about my teacher Miss Hyles, the headmistress at Little Ness school, whom we called Hyler.

"She talcum-powders her toes on arriving at school. Pulls on spare socks and a pair of polished shoes for indoor use. Stokes up the fire."

"Keeps a green ashplant in a high lop-lidded desk, also reserved for registers and other strong documents. Stained, astringent-smelling drawers whizz open in her marking table as she thrusts the chair back and wrestles with hard answer-books, red pens, needles, cotton reels, thimbles, clips and scissors. She deftly picks a spare hairpin out, claps the clips and scissors back, scratches her head and drums a pen handle on the offending exercise book."

"Takes off to attend to the fire; then to knitting: clickety-click . . . another pair of over-socks for winter

34

insulation. 'Turn another heel for walking at weekends and seal the inlets to oneself'. "

John sealed the inlets round his ears.

Words are part of an older brother's armoury. Silence is another. There is a third. You, the younger one, are walking along, lagging as usual, slightly behind. You see something, an ash fork for a catapult perhaps. You say, "Look, John." He says, "I'm looking," yet he marches steadfastly on, his head in the air, eyes front, like a boy scout on parade. What is more, you know he is not interested in your "catty fang" because he has made umpteen catapults before, bound them with string, seasoned them in a low oven, thonged them with soft leather and slung them with that tough, square, black elastic which is only obtainable from certain tobacconists in town. He thinks you are going to ask him to help you with it. You wouldn't mind, of course. But you know he has left you behind and you will never catch up . . .

I fell asleep.

In the morning, John was, as usual, up first and under the pump. He spent an hour attending to his ferrets and going round his rabbit traps.

I didn't have to milk but I still had my chickens to feed. I had some pullets of my own. Of all the animals on the farm, wild or domesticated, I preferred the feathered kind. Except of course for Topsy, who generally looked after herself.

At a quarter to eight or thereabouts, Mother dressed by the fire. (She was usually dressing by the fire behind the screen when the postman put his head round the door and called, "Can ya 'ear me, Muther!" "Cheeky devil," muttered Mother, feet caught in her coms.) Breakfast should have been ready at eight, but this particular spring morning it was not. We could not get the fire to draw. I had to hold the paper in front. Then, whoosh, the paper caught light and flew up the chimney, flames and all. When we did get it going, John got a cuff on the ear for not taking the kettle off before it boiled over, filling the hearth with a pall of hissing smoke and steam. Dad came in from milking with a "Who's douted the fire?" Mother replied with a carefully aimed "Breakfast will be ten minutes late." And John resigned himself to missing the "buz".

We lived in a world of doubtful fears and certainties. If we douted the fire we made a good job of putting it out. Do out equals dout. And if we said we doubted we'd missed the bus we were certain sure we had.

John would have to cycle seven and a half miles to school in Shrewsbury. We had only fifty yards to walk; and still we trooped in late.

"You live on top of the school!" Miss Hyles greeted us with more force than accuracy, I thought. I was sorry because if I had been earlier I might have been asked to choose the hymn. And it would not have been "My God how wonderful thou art" or "Oft in danger oft in woe". I chose hymns which I had learnt at choir practice with notes that Miss Heavens, who was also the leading singer in the choir, had a struggle to reach. My favourites were the Easter Alleluias, dismissed as "out of season now". And there was "Ten thousand times ten thousand", which left me breathlessly singing solo in verse three of "knitting severed friendships up, where partings are no more". No wonder I was bullied.

After a quick request to God who had safely brought us to the beginning of this day, to defend us in the same, we set about arithmetic. Practice, the Method of Unity and the Rule of Three.

"Six is to eighteen as twenty is to what?"

"Um . . ."

"Multiply the eighteen by the twenty; divide the answer by the six and what do you get?"

"Sixty, Miss."

"Now go away and do the rest."

Hyler's motto, if she had one, was "Make haste, and do it quickly. Cover the ground!" But I made heavy weather of Practice, the Method of Unity and the Rule of Three and by playtime I had only half-finished the exercise.

"Stay in!" Outside I could hear raucous voices of full-throated fourteen-year-olds (the senior boys) slaughtering the innocents. It was a question of which was worse: beating one's head inside on the abstract Rule of Three or having it beaten outside on the concrete playground earth. The escape route to the grammar school, though difficult, was there. John was one of the few who had managed it. But, to my eleven-year-old mind, it sometimes seemed preferable to be a dunce and stick it out at Little Ness for three more years, then kick the dust of school right off my feet on someone else's head!

After play, however, instead of Peterborough, Petersfield and Peterhead — the places that interested me in my geography book — we were given a really original assignment: a study of "Our Village".

"You've seen the yellow AA sign on Mr Martin's wall. A hundred and sixty-two miles to London, ninety-nine to Holyhead. How many miles is it to Shrewsbury, Jimmy?"

"Sev'n'arf, Miss."

"Seven and a half. And three to Baschurch. There you are." She gave out generous helpings of drawing paper. "Start with the sign; colour it and write all you can about your village and what we call the neighbourhood. And draw a big map. You may find it is not such a little village after all."

"Wow!" We made a great yellow sun and put Little Ness on the equator of the world. All other places were of secondary importance. We were on the map. What was more, we were allowed to continue with the project at home. I too had homework. This really would make John sit up in bed.

After grace ("These creatures bless and grant that we may feast in Paradise with Thee") we poured out to play, and lunch. I envied those who had their lunch at school. The older lads climbed to the top of the oak tree by the pit and cast their crumbs down on the juveniles who struggled to find a perch below. We, who lived only a step from the school, looked for bats which sometimes hung upside down on the rutted bark or tried to find a four-leaf clover in the grass. We called up names to the bullies above, who could only splutter between mouthfuls: "F — awf, Davy duck, stuck in the muck. Go 'n get yer babbies' milk."

"Shut yer cake 'ole, Drippin' Tin."

Mother was late with the lunch that day. We trailed back to school, shame-faced but safe, and missed "May manna to our souls be given; the bread of life sent down from heaven." I still had my Practice, the Method of Unity and the ROT to finish. There was reading, during which, if teacher had given us a ten, we took it up to the head boy, Bobby Chesney, who recorded it with his fountain pen in a notebook which was a sight for a bullied boy's sore eyes. Bobby's red hair caught the sun and seemed to go with his royal blue writing and all those royal blue regular ones and noughts. Dorothy, the head girl sitting next to him, quietly slipped her arm round his blue jersey to show that she went with him too. The old clock ticked on the wall above the fire. Teacher, knitting, turned a heel. The girls busied themselves with button holes, stitched nightdresses of rosebud flannelette or summer frocks of fragrant cotton print. I went with *Black Beauty* into peaceful retirement from Practice, the Method of Unity and the Rule of Three.

"Playtime's late." My neighbour Jim passed wind, noisily, as he did everything: reading and the passing of remarks. You could not get too near to Jim. His corner in the cloakroom smelt like a ferret hutch. He had hair like coconut matting, no handkerchief and dirt-retentive ears. But it was good to have him as a buffer against the bullies in the playground.

"You'll have your games after," announced Miss Hyles, starting another row.

She knitted all through games. We played rounders and I missed a catch off Big Fat Jelly Rump, which meant that Bob, my captain, would turn a blind eye when BFJR nailed me next.

First home from school at half past three, I opened the back door to an irate "Who is that?"

"It's me — er — It is I." Mother, even on her knees, was a stickler for grammar.

"Just keep your eye on that kettle. And tell me when it's four o'clock. Where are those girls?"

"With Florrie in the quarry."

"I'll give them Florrie in the quarry when I get hold of them." She scraped the bucket over the stone floor and wrung the floor cloth out. A huge network of veins swelled in her arms. Sweat ran from her face. She peeled a length of hair off her cheek. She looked exhausted. "What time is it?"

"It's ten to four."

Once a week, as regular as clockwork, and just as unwelcome, came the vicar. Other afternoons Mother could listen to the play on the wireless. Gladys Young, Belle Crystal, Grizelda Harvey and the young Marjorie Westbury came in over the air and helped her solve or shelve the problems of debt, damp, dilapidation, drudgery and disease. But for Mr Parrott she had to be "dressed and tidy". After she had set a tray with the best china and thinly sliced bread and butter, she washed herself. She could not even do as she did on Saturdays and say, "There's the bus. Go and tell him I'm just putting my hat on." (Him was not the bus, but Mr Waggs the driver. And she was not just putting her hat on but washing her "under-beneath".)

Precisely on the dot of four the knocker sounded. Mother had made the tea. "Go on now. Let him in!" It was a long way to the front door.

"Good afternoon, sir."

He stepped inside. "Ah, Mrs Davies, how d'you do?"

I went outside to feed the fowl and to collect the eggs. An early broody hen showed some annoyance on the nest. I pitched her off. The cockerel flew at me. I struck him with the keys. He lay spread-eagled on the grass.

"So what did Mr Parrott want?" I asked later, as if I cared.

"The free-will offering is due." Mother screwed her cigarette end into the visitors' ashtray and turned her back on charity. "You'd better get the cows in soon. Your father's not come home. Ask Emrys next door to help you to milk. John will have his homework to do. He can feed the pigs and shut the poultry up."

"I'll shut —"

"You'll what?"

"— the fold gate up. Dad always says it's the most important thing to do at night." My offer must have sounded weak.

"You don't like shutting the fowl up in winter, so why are you so concerned now? I'll get John to do it. Foxes are hungry now. They have their cubs to feed."

41

That was my Achilles heel: my fear of the dark. We had lost hens before because I did not shut them up. Beautiful pullets, just coming into lay, all strewn around with their heads bitten off . . . Mother knew me better than I knew myself. I needed someone to watch over me. And Emrys came, singing and smiling, as unconcerned by trouble as a jocund troubadour. The cows, from "ballocking" at the gate — their milk straining from distended teats — came in quietly, thankfully, and settled down to an extra allowance of cake. Milk purred in the pail. The cat, sitting upright, trimmed its bib and roped its feet round with its tail. Motes of dust still swung in sunlight from the west.

"Less than a month and it'll be the longest day," said Emrys.

"Can't be much longer than this," said I.

It was late, for me, when I went up to bed that night. "You asleep?" I asked John.

"Yes."

"What relation is Emrys to next door?"

"A younger brother."

"He's not like them."

"You're not like me."

"I wish I lived next door." There was no sound from John, but a faint susurration under the sheets. John was indulging in a new solo bedtime occupation. Counting up to a million. "What's after a million?" I asked.

"A billion."

"And after a billion?"

"A trillion."

"And after that?"

No answer, then: "A shitty-ga-lillion!"

We were forced to smother our laughter, doubled up in our sheets. We heard Dad going to bed. He coughed. The wooden stairs creaked under his unsteady tread. Woodbine smoke stained the night air.

COLOURFUL FRIENDS

At least three people we knew, apart from Uncle Archie, had crossed the Atlantic: Dick Bromley, John Thonger and Jack Birch. They took pedigree Hereford cattle, tending them on their long voyages, to pastures in the New World.

Jack Birch lived at The Shruggs, which is just what the name suggests: a shrug of hill and woodland, crested like a wild pony's mane. A frontier outpost in the early days, it lay between the Cliffe and Nesscliffe Hill, snugly concealed, away from the Severn and the Holyhead road. A sandy track ran where roots of pine, beech, holly and larch spread hands to grasp a limestone anchorage, tufted with heather, bracken and gorse. Along that track, in the desperate times following 1929, Jack had built a sheet-iron shack for his family of many children and a shed for two cows.

"The Birches' world," said John, "makes Huck Finn's look sophisticated."

Jack Birch remembered the rabbits were different in the States: "They called 'em jack rabbits," he said.

Jack's second son, Harry, was John's special friend. He was big for his age, good-looking, rode a black pony Dolly, bare-back and bridleless, "hell for leather" round their hedgeless field that backed onto a plantation of larch; kept ferrets in hutches by the house; and had once fallen out of the walnut tree and hung by one ear from a nail in the trunk. With Harry's help, John might begin to get rich. But Harry was too impatient, he said; too feckless to learn the difficult art of snaring rabbits. You had to study their runs.

"Rabbits have habits," he said. The rabbits we saw in the fields did not hop aimlessly about. Their runs are especially noticeable at certain times of the year: early autumn, for example; and, later, at the time of the first frosts. Harry did not have John's science or art or craft. Harry preferred to use his lurcher, Spike — a cross between a greyhound and something wire-haired and horrible — too tall to catch a rabbit and not manoeuvrable enough to catch a hare. John's own dog, Gyp, was neater, nimbler, more intelligent. He had given the gypsies five shillings for him and a packet of Woodbines, as a pup. Not to be compared with the spiky mongrel, more like a dusty doormat at The Shruggs than a real half-crown earning asset, John said. And Harry kept ferrets, again, not so much to use as to trade for other ferrets or lurcher pups or a 2.2 rifle. John, on the other hand, would wait by a burrow for hours for a lost ferret, sometimes till late at night. Once, he was working the top field burrows by a yew at the corner of the churchyard. He saw a tombstone move. He ran like the wind.

"Harry's not a sticker," he said. "He delights to take up an idea for a time if it offers gain without pain." Not a bully in any violent way, but when he wanted my superior catapult, made by a young gypsy, he forced it from me, trading his own for it in a heavy, sullen, boring way . . .

Poor John! Poor Harry!

John kept me awake at night with his stories, like this one he called "An Ash Tree Struck by Lightning".

In a field between the near side of the — Legs and the coppy stood a sixty-foot ash tree. Alas, it stands no more. Harry Birch and I caused it to lie down. This is the true story of how it happened.

Our father and Jack Birch of The Shruggs had secret deposits of empty beer bottles here, there and everywhere. Harry and I used to take them in sacks to either the Old Three Pigeons' Inn or the Nesscliffe Hotel and get the money back. On one occasion we crossed the field by the ash tree and set down our load in the shade. I noticed the rabbit holes between the roots and suggested to Harry, who liked a smoke, that he would do well to smoke the rabbits out. We could then sell them to increase our profit. We stuffed newspaper in the sacks between the bottles to stop them clanking. This we put in the holes with dry twigs and ignited it. A merry blaze ensued. No rabbits, however, jumped out. The venture was deemed a failure by Harry, who was keen to get to the pub.

Hours after selling our cargo at Nesscliffe Hotel, we retraced our steps. We looked in vain for the sixty-foot tree. Only when we reached the hedge did we see it lying on the ground, a wisp of smoke escaping from a rabbit hole.

Harry, of all our friends, was most like Huckleberry Finn. His father, Jack, was famously strong. He once got his pony and cart stuck in a pond at Great Ness, waded in up to his armpits, loosed the chains so that the pony could swim to safety, then dragged the cart out with his own two hands. Lizzie, his wife, helped Mother in the house, especially on pig-killing days. "Nothing but the squeal is wasted," she would say, bringing a brawny arm over her face, dripping with steam and sweat. "Of a pig," she would add. Her iron-grey hair, scraped back in a bun, always escaped from the pins that, like iron hurdles, fenced it in. You could bet your bottom dollar on Lizzie making a good job of a pig. Then, one day to everyone's surprise, something incredible happened.

It was washday. Lizzie had not come to help Mother. The red-brick floor of our kitchen sank under the weight of the mangle, which stood like an animal, immovable in strong carbolic swill. The windows steamed. Our mother steamed. The kettle thrummed on the hob.

"No, you can't have a drink yet . . . No, tea's not ready yet. You can feed the fowl."

Damp, ruffled hens on perches in the henhouse, tails down . . . Few eggs that day. Chuck corn on floor, among dirt . . . Hens not house-proud.

"Not many eggs today."

"I can't help that. Leave what you've got by the sink. And leave your boots outside."

46

Then, just before nightfall, Lizzie came puffing in from The Shruggs, breathless and somehow impervious to rain.

"What do you think?" she said. "Our Harry's joined the Black Watch!"

"Never!" said Mother.

"'E 'as — an I'd like you to see 'im in 'is kilt! Now, while 'e's at 'ome an' the pub's closed!" With that she was gone, grey overall flapping, grey hair escaping out of its pins, plump as a wood-pigeon, flying down the lane.

Next morning, very early, I ran down the fields to the fowlhouse and opened the bob-hole. Out sprang fifty flighty Leghorns like fifty brides in white. Out swept the cock and married them in the grass. I watched them dip and let him tread on them, or swerve and make him spin around and rasp his wing and fan it out against his spurs. Some led him off to breakfast on a worm.

Back at the house, I took a bowl of Force flakes and skimmed the cream off last night's milk. After the steely air of the fields the house smelt closed-up, sour, bad. Stale vapours of whisky thickened with smoke hung round the stairs and varnished cellar door. How I hated that cellar door! By the screen, by the fireplace, stood an empty bottle and my father's boots. In the sitting-room I fingered through my sheaf of homework papers, blank as yet except for one gold sun. Mother passed by with the slop pail in one hand, a damp cloth in the other. Dead matches floated on the slops. "The old cock's in. You'd better start the milking anyway. He may not come round for a while."

Was it with relief that she said the old cock's in? I never really knew. And the doubts and fears that darkened our lives prevented us from fully stating anything. We smiled, but we didn't really share the joke. Never a close-knit family in any overt sense, we touched each other only when we came to blows. We all quarrelled with one another: the girls because the younger one was spoilt, and I with my twin Laura if only to magnify the co-operative hell we could let loose if anyone went for either of us. And Dad and Mother often came to blows. For Dad didn't know what I know now: that women seek domination over men. "I'm the master in this house!" she'd shout, and Dad would hit her all about the head. Once I saw him strike her, head down over the side oven while she basted the meat with scalding fat; and still she held on to the tin.

I set about the milking, easy now the grass was good. There was no hay to carry in; no mucking out. Just seven sleek udders oozing milk; seven pairs of liquid eyes and seven warm, sweet, mealy breaths. Sometimes the cow would cough and, dreaming, you would drop the pail, or she would draw a sloppy tail across your face. That stopped the clock. All else was soothing as the milk sang in the pail. I did my thinking then.

I thought about my project. How would I picture Little Ness? Not with dark photographs of a dog-toothed Norman arch . . . I thought of the river, the Perry, and the time I saw a stallion get across it to a mare and what a fight went on. Cocks and hens didn't squeal and fight like that. Cows didn't. They did it to each other — for pleasure, it seemed. Our dog did it to the pigs.

The whiff of a Woodbine, the scrape of my father's boots on the cobbles, the clank of another pail, startled me. Dad had his milking cap round the wrong way, an inch of ash on his cigarette, his boots unlaced and combinations struggling out below his breeches. He took his stool and started drumming loudly on the bottom of the pail. His stroke was strong. When he put his mind to it he could beat anybody at milking, breaking a horse, judging cattle . . . He was the best "grower of pigs" in the district.

"Where's the River Perry come from, Dad?"

"Up above Os'estry." He talked from behind his cigarette.

"Go on."

"Oh, Baggymoor, the Lees, up Wykey way —" He coughed and had to stop his steady pumping in the pail. "By Wigmarsh, where you used to live. Yo ask Miss Hyles. It goes on down by Grafton where 'er lives."

"But where exactly does it rise?"

"Yo ask at school. Yer feyther never went to school."

"You did!"

"Not all that much. Not all that long, I didn't. Tommy got his schoolin' in the yeomanry. Whatever 'e learnt, 'e learnt with the hosses. It rises in the sky."

My father was a fine man really. His conversation, like his manner, was by turns rough, subtle, shrewd and amusing, depending on the time of day and company.

He viewed the world through long-sighted, half-closed eyes and a cloud of Woodbine smoke.

When the cowhouse door was open we could see across the orchard to the Chapel Meadow. The school caretaker, a little bent figure in black, retraced her steps to her home by the church. A spiral of smoke mounted from the chimney of the school.

"'Er means to be warm, 'tany rate." He meant Miss Hyles, who kept a good fire going — whatever the weather. "I reckon 'er's got an allowance for coal."

When I arrived at school at five to nine the fire was gleaming in the grate; and gleaming on my sheaf of papers, golden sun and two words: Little Ness.

It was the Diocesan Scripture Examination that day. We were at it at school all morning. First we had Prayers. Then we sang "Do no sinful action". Then we did sums while the vicar and someone called the Archdemon went to the infants and asked them all about love. Then they came to us. And we started with Latin.

"Rogationtide . . . *Rogare* is a Latin word. It means 'to ask'. We ask a blessing on the crops; and on the fruits of God's Holy Spirit working within us. Which, I wonder, do you suppose is the most important of all the Church's feasts?"

"Communion, sir?"

"No, not exactly, Jimmy. You're thinking of eating, aren't you now? No, not Communion. Who can name me a feast? Well, when was Jesus born? Tommy?"

"'tChristmas, sir."

"And when did He rise from the dead?"

50

"'tEaster, sir."

"And when did He ascend into Heaven?"

"'tAscension, sir."

"And when did God send His Holy Spirit?"

"'tWhitsun, sir."

"Yes, Pentecost. Now, which of those feasts or festivals do you think is the most important?"

"Harvest, sir?"

"No, Dozy, you weren't listening!"

"Er, Christmas, sir?"

"No."

"Easter, sir?"

"No."

"Ascension, sir?"

"No."

"Whitsun, sir?"

"*Yes!*"

Then we went on to the Sacraments, the whole way through. We went right through the catechism — not just bits of it, but all of it.

"What is thy duty towards thy neighbour, Peter Davies?" The vicar stood before me, pink and white.

"My duty towards my neighbour is to love him as myself, and to do to all men . . . my father and mother . . . to love, no, honour and obey the King" — who looked down from his portrait on the wall — "to submit myself to all my governors, teachers" — Miss Hyles looked up with big, brown eyes — "spiritual pastors" — "And masters," added Mr Parrott — "to order myself lowly and reverently to all my betters" — that must be why we touched our caps — "to hurt

51

nobody" — that meant I mustn't hit Jimmy Roberts — "to be true and just" — it was getting harder and harder — "in all my dealing. To keep my hands from picking and stealing, and my tongue from evil-speaking, lying and slandering."

I wasn't allowed to go on to my body because Jimmy Roberts reminded everyone that I had missed out the bit about malice an' 'atred in my 'eart.

"Go on then, Jimmy." Mr Parrott cunningly controlled the flow.

"To keep my body in temperance, soberness, an' chastity — nottocovetnordesire-othermen'sgoods-butto-labour —"

"Learn, Jimmy."

"— learnan'labour —"

"Slowly, Jimmy . . ." The parson accompanied us through to the end and we then rounded it off with a rousing Amen.

"No," said Mr Parrott, "no Amen."

In the Lord's Prayer a chilblain burst in my shoe. My impetigo sore itched on my knee. We were all bothered with boils. If this was the state of my body, whatever was happening to my soul? I must keep my hands from picking my scab and bear no malice or hatred in my heart.

In the afternoon Miss Hyles told us all the things we did wrong. But she said that I had answered very well, and Jimmy whispered, "Clever dick."

We said "Lighten our darkness" and I went home with my golden sun a little dimmed.

Seeking inspiration I went into the sitting-room, to the cupboard full of books. I spotted a slender brown volume with no title on its spine. I took it down from the shelf to find the front cover simply inscribed in capital letters: LITTLE NESS.

Closer examination revealed that the author was the Reverend P.A. Parrott and that it was dedicated to the loved and honoured memory of his mother. "Ask now of the days that are past" the inscription read. The text was scholarly and rather dense, but here and there I picked out a sentence that shone like a crystal in a dull heap of earth. I began to see our sober village, not as a place that had always been the same, but as part of the moving pageant of the past. Celtic troops tramped over it. Skinclad traders rolled their ox carts through the riverside morning mists. The earl lieutenants of the marches picked out Nesse for their demesne. The Conqueror rewarded Roger de Montgomery with it as part of the great manor of Oswestry and Clun.

Mr Parrott revealed the meanings of the names of some of our familiar fields: Chapel Meadow, Mill Meadow, The Leasowes, Tinker's Field, Rushy Meadow, Old Ryegrass, Clover Piece, Hemp Butt, Flaxyards . . . I glowed with pride at sight of them. I imagined the weavers' cottages occupied by shawled figures bent over looms and spinning wheels, producing linen from the flax by rush-light, late at night.

"The Cock-pit" conjured up cock fights held "in the days when this form of sport was numbered among the pleasures of princes". The pound, the Pinfold, was where the school is now!

"Ness," Mr Parrott explained, meant a headland; but our parish took its name from the hill overlooking the Perry which had been an ancient castle site. The earthwork had enclosed, beside the castle, the mound which was believed to be the burial place of Celtic Prince Kyndylan. The church — in which Mr Parrott was naturally most interested — had been built, he said, "within the cincture of the court". That phrase, "within the cincture of the court", sang in my brain. However bloody the final battle had been, Kyndylan, I thought, could not have found a more peaceful place to rest.

My mother's voice broke up my reverie. "You haven't touched the piano all week," she shouted from the wash tub.

"Right." I rattled off the "Soldier's March" and "The Wild Horseman" and settled down to "Dreaming" (*Traumerei*). That always humoured her.

"Not so much of the loud pedal," she yelled.

Then my younger sister Belle brought her friend Glad-eyes in from school. She played "The Wild Horseman" even faster than I did and, feeling beaten, I left the field to her. Mother, still doing some washing in the kitchen, said I could help Laura, who was weeding the little yard.

Living as we did in an old farmhouse, surrounded by battered out-buildings full of death traps and hell holes, it was no wonder Mother sometimes gave us the endless task of weeding the little yard. She could, if she had a spare moment, peer through the steamed-up kitchen window and count us — one, two, three, four

— in our cords or sloppy pinafores (like prisoners out at exercise) toiling with broken, yellow-handled kitchen knives, digging up the grass that grew between the cobblestones. It came up easily after rain, the soil on the roots, like pieces of cake. In a dry spell it was painful to knuckles and knees and strained the insteps of your feet. The knives grated on the stones and set your teeth on edge.

Mother had been informed by letter that day that Laura and I had gained our scholarships to the Priory School in Shrewsbury, in September. Instead of rejoicing at the prospect, Laura was sobbing softly to herself. "You'll have a new bike," I said to cheer her up. "I'll have to have John's old Coventry Eagle — but I shan't mind."

"I don't want to go."

"Go and do the fowl then," Mother called from the window, "and don't forget to give them some water."

"I'll help you," I said; and we went together with buckets of corn and water round the farm and collected the eggs. Hens ranged everywhere. They laid away: in the hedges, in the stackyard and in buildings wherever they found some straw. In one of the lofts we found a cock egg, a tiny thing, the last of the line before a hen starts to brood; a little fairy thing, useless and infertile, but enchanting and quite unknown to many people who think they know about eggs.

"There you are," I said, "you can throw it over the house and make a wish."

That day a tiny builderman, whom Mother had nicknamed Little Tich, was busy on his ladder at the never-ending job of replacing the wind-blown roofing slates. He descended his ladder wiping his moustache with his forefinger and shaking the slimy egg white off his hand. "That was a funny egg," he said. "It hadn't got a yolk!"

In the secrecy of the bedchamber a few nights later John and I explored the little brown book. There was a great deal about the church, its surrounding sandstone walls and overhanging dark old yew trees, sinister and dense.

"Listen to this," said John, his flashlamp lighting up the sheet drawn over his head like a tent. "'It would be interesting to excavate the Tumulus at Little Ness and to discover what (if anything) is hidden beneath; but perhaps it is wiser to let the mound keep its secret, and reverence it as a hallowed spot where the last Welsh Lord of Pengwern Powys may have received a hurried and blood-stained burial.'"

Mr Parrott went on to tell of an avaricious person who, long ago, dug into the tumulus for supposed hidden treasure. After much labour, the man came upon an immense chest, the lid of which was no sooner uncovered than it lifted itself up a little, and out sprang an enormous black cat, which seated itself upon the chest and glowed with eyes of passion upon the intruder. The man tried to move the chest. He fixed an enormous chain to it and attached a team of powerful horses. The chain broke in a hundred pieces, and the chest disappeared for ever.

"It's as good as *The Tinder Box*," said I.

"Or *The Hound of the Baskervilles*," said John.

We always knew our mound was special. More overhanging yew trees glowered round its edge and one rose like a ship's mast from the top, tortured and terrifying on a moonlit, windy night. No cats sprang out, but rabbits did. And ferrets, sometimes lost in the burrows there, came out with pleasure and satisfaction in their little pink eyes. The trouble was it lay in alien ground. It had been enclosed by the neighbouring farmer who was indeed a Welshman and a Nonconformist. We little Anglican Saxons were occasionally hauled up before the blind headman to answer for our predatory misdeeds.

"Hey, look at this!" John then yelled. "A murder!"

I hurried over to John's bed to see what he had found. The words bobbed up and down in the flashlight's beam.

"'The inhabitants of Little Ness,'" John read, "'were stirred in 1863 by the news of a very brutal murder committed in the parish of Baschurch. About the year 1857, Edward Cooper, a labourer, was living in Church Lane. His wife having died, he tried to find lodging in Valeswood for his two young infant sons; but the elder one was deformed and thought to have a disease, so he could not be taken in. The man was keeping company with a servant maid at Red House . . .'" John was skipping it, and lowering his voice.

"Don't leave any out!" I thumped him on the arm. It was like hitting a branch of a tree.

"He tried to send his boy to the workhouse . . . but he only earned five bob . . ."

"It doesn't say that. Read it properly!" I twisted his ear.

"'With his eight-year-old son he walked to Hanwood to visit relatives, but failed to get them to take the boy in. On the way back to Baschurch, where he was working at the time, they passed through the Ash Coppice, on the Baschurch side of the Perry stream. Here Cooper strangled the boy, and borrowing a spade from a cottage nearby, he buried the boy in the wood. The disappearance of the boy aroused suspicions . . . the wood was searched . . . disturbed earth was dug and the boy's body revealed. Cooper was arrested while ploughing near Ellesmere . . . The trial took place at the Shropshire Lent Assize and after ten hours he was condemned to death. A scaffold was erected over the entrance to the county gaol and a crowd of ten thousand witnessed the execution on eleventh April, 1863. The last public execution but one held at Shrewsbury.'"

"There," said John, "put that in your village book."

I didn't think I could. But I had news for Jimmy Roberts and the other boys at school in the morning!

I borrowed the fading flash to find my way back to my bed. Pulling the sheets tightly over my head, I wrapped myself uneasily in a ragged veil of sleep.

The story of the murder was all round school next day. All through the Sons of Jacob and the Tribes of Israel Jimmy kept whispering behind his hand: "Go on . . . What else?" And Hyler said, "Whispering's rude." Len

Watkins leant over to hear what we were talking about so that he could tell Bobby Chesney.

"Listeners hear no good of themselves!" Hyler was growing alarmed. And when the words Red House, Valeswood, the workus and Soosbury gaol got round the class she shouted, "Empty vessels make most sound!"

"Keep quiet, or we'll have to write it out!" I said. And Jimmy made a sound suggesting he was full.

During the Friday test, of course, no one was allowed to talk. "It's murder," muttered Jim . . .

Released at last at half past ten, I claimed my wide-mouthed, captivated audience. Never was there such stillness in the boys' yard at that hour. Never before, and never again.

"Them maids am a rum lot at Red 'Ouse!" said one who knew. His father was the waggoner. Nobody knew any Coopers so somebody, heartless, said they'd all died out. We wondered where the boy had gone to stay in Valeswood. "To nurse, did ya say?"

"It might a bin down at your house, Jim," I said. "Under the Cliffe."

"Or more like down at Startlewood," said Jim. "Yo da know what them lot does, stuck away down theer!"

"But where was the workhouse?" Kenny Neate asked. He spoke polite. He had a lot of tens in his book.

"The only workus as I knows of 's at Morda, Os'estry," said Big Fat Jelly Rump — quite friendly like. But then went on, "Or Shelton?"

"No, that's the loony bin, ya foo-ool," Doug Evans shrieked through shattered, gappy teeth.

"Sooner!" "Ass!" and "Drip!" the chorus swelled.

But Puggy Pugh was serious: "Weer's that coppy, weer 'e buried 'im? Ash Coppy, did ya say?"

"I think I know," said Copperknob, a little freckled boy whose address was simply "down the fi'lds". "My uncle knows the cottage where he got the spade. It's up across them fi'lds not far frum Baschurch church."

"Fancy them 'angin' a man at Soosbury gaol!" said Butchie Humphreys.

"Surry ah, an' over the gate! An' all them gawpers gawpin' on!"

Glyn Jones, who was good at drawing, said he'd do a picture of it in his village book.

"Capital idea," said Hyler, who didn't ring the bell. We were having such a good discussion; worthwhile, friendly too, she said. But soon she reminded us that we still had to do our maps.

"Please, Miss, I can't find Little Ness on the map." Jimmy spoke for all of us. "Then *put* it on the map!" was Hyler's clear, unhelpful reply. Back in the classroom we were fired with an unholy zeal. And Hyler roused herself with a "There's the river!" She quickly drew a squiggle down the blackboard from the top left corner to the bottom right. "Somewhere down there it joins the Severn." She swept the Severn out of Wales across the bottom of the blackboard with a spluttering of exploding chalk. "Baschurch is north of the Perry. Little Ness, and our road, to the south. Right in the middle. There." She marked it L.N. "Now put in some fields."

I knew the fields along the river well: all those fertile fields that had, as Mr Parrott said, a rich subsoil of loam. I'd made a start. Fields, green and golden, in irregular shapes and sizes, all dotted with trees and trimmed with hedges, filled my page. The road ran south and nearly parallel to the river from Ruyton-XI-Towns to Montford Bridge. I marked the school. I marked my house.

That night John gave me help with my map. His new Philip's atlas was strong, he said, on the physical side. (I liked the political maps with their multicoloured county patchworks: pink for Shropshire, yellow for Leicestershire, green for Kent and red for Devon — no one knew why.) His atlas had a whole page devoted to Shropshire, heavily scored with deep brown markings like the knotted graining on our cellar door. We lay prone in bed with the atlas and the little brown book spread out on the pillow, and the flashlamp in John's hand.

"You haven't put in the post office" was John's immediate complaint. "You've got to think of people. Where does everybody go? Not to church. They go to the post office. Or even if they don't, they may get a letter. Why don't you go round with the postman? That's it! Take the letters round. Now, where would you start? At the Red House! 'Mr F. Davies, a letter for you'." He made it sound like a play.

I realized then how many miles our postman rode on his sturdy bicycle with the carrier mounted on the front and his bag slung over his back. He must have gone from the post office to the cottages down Church Lane.

People at the Bottom Buildings, the Foxholes and World's End probably didn't receive many letters. Then back to Red House, Little Ness House, the Chesneys, on down to Adcote Mill. Then round by Quality Square, to Nibs Heath, back to the square and the Home Farm. Then Lower House, Church House, the Parsonage, to Valeswood and back. Then miles along the Ruyton road, where he lived, for a rest! I wrote it all out, added a map and handed it in on Monday morning with "All things bright and beautiful."

Hyler said I was covering the ground.

CHAPTER
TWO

Excursions
Near and Far

It was soon half-term: "Teacher's rest and Mother's pest," as someone said. But Mother had her children organized. We were going to Baschurch, to see Uncle Percy, Auntie Mary and favourite cousin Margery at the Corner Stores.

"*Tout de suite!*" our mother sang. She was airing her French. "*Allez-vous en.*" My hair was smudged with blue-green brilliantine. I slid down the banisters, sickening myself on the knob at the bottom, skidded on the polished floor in the hall, banged the front door behind me, raced down the garden path and beat my brother who came smelling of ferrets from the back. Mother at the front gate grabbed my ear. "Your hair's a state! You look like a gypsy!" She spat on her hankie and prodded my ear. "And please breathe through your nose. You've been to Caroline?"

"*Tout de suite!*" With neat and purposefully pointed feet, she set out for Baschurch with her ill-assorted brood, more easily driven than led. Passing the Red House on our left and Little Ness House on our right, we almost tiptoed past the Chesneys' house, hoping that Bobby and Vic would not hear our mother *tout-de-suiting* and cackling her *allez-vous-ens*. Eileen, the girl, was in the garden flashing her brilliant white teeth and looking every inch a tennis player, a scholarship winner, a champion swimmer, a brilliant dancer . . . Eileen excelled in everything. The boys, as it happened, were absorbed, heads down, in the mesmeric process of still further refining their racing bicycles. Each one of these machines was so light that you could balance it on an out-stretched forefinger; wheels so free and frictionless they spun continuously in the air. Dedicated mechanics, the Chesneys, it seemed, were on the verge of discovering the secret of perpetual motion. I continued to walk on my toes downhill, thinking I might learn to walk — and run — like a pony. I had tried leaping off walls and learning to fly. Now I wanted only to run as fast as Topsy or Dorothy May, the ponies we had left at home in the field.

"What are you trying to do now? Wear your shoes out?" Mother didn't understand. I would have taken my shoes off, but then I would have worn out my socks. I went on stubbing my toes and puffing up dust.

"Les Spence has got a baby sister," John whispered as we approached Adcote where Les lived.

"No!" said I.

"It's a fact!" said he.

(We talked just like Dad when a dealer came to the farm and told him what had topped the market, a Friesian cow perhaps, and how much it had made. "No!" said Dad. "It's a fact!" said he.)

"Where did he get it from?" asked Belle, who heard everything as usual.

"Under the gooseberry bush," said Mother.

"That's why he's keeping quiet about it then," said John.

We passed the Adcote turn, the Lodge, the coppice of spruce, and the string of chestnut horses netted with veins and tormented by flies. "They're blood horses," John said loftily. I had heard of horses bursting blood vessels. Their vessels all looked so near the surface, the thought of them bursting was so painful I accelerated out of range. At Milford we stopped by the bridge. Soon we were hanging head down over the sandstone parapet, looking for fish and chewing long, sweet, juicy stems of grass. Sunbeams danced and rippled on our arms as we hugged the warm and friendly stone. We passed from speech and thought to something more like revelation.

"It was born at home . . ."

"It didn't come from the hospital . . ."

"It came out of Mrs Spence. That's what."

"*Dépêchez-vous!*" Our rest was over. We struck across the fields. A whiff of steam. The steady thud of traction engines gave new life to flagging limbs. "There's Baschurch church!" Before the church we passed the Ash Coppice.

"That's where Cooper did the murder," said John.

"I'll race you to the church," said I.

The church wall scaled, we waited for Mother, who had to go by way of the stile. She was squatting like a partridge in the grass, "minding her own business", as she said. The old red sandstone church, looking as solid as a barracks, protested with a peal of bells.

"They'll see you from the tower."

"They ring them from the floor," said Mother, unperturbed.

"It's a wedding," yelled my sisters. "Can we watch?" A crowd of people had gathered by the lych gate to see the bride arrive: a tiny fleck of white, a chaffinch in a crowd of crows.

We staggered up the village street past butchers' shops smelling of scrubbed wood and sawdust till we reached our uncle's shop. "To sweets!" we cried. No spurs were needed now; no tired tags of French.

The shop was closed. It was Uncle Percy's half-day. He was sitting with his feet up, smoking his pipe. Aunt Mary was washing up. Cousin Margery was doing somebody's hair in the village. Belle, Laura and I went into the garden: I to study the early apples, particularly the Beauty of Bath, they the three-holed lavatory seat. John stayed in the house reading *Self Help* by Samuel Smiles. Mother was drinking tea.

"An apple isn't ripe till it comes off in your hand . . ." Echoes of Old Testament wisdom puffed from behind my uncle's pipe fell on my inner ear. "It should come off of its own accord. You only need to put your hand under it and cradle it, like a baby." Conscience said Shut up! I pretended to myself that I walked alone in the garden. "Like an egg . . . No use if you drop it."

I tested the nearest. The test didn't work. I climbed the tree. A man was taking a wheel off a car. He wore an oily overall, so I supposed it was all right; but I had never seen a man taking a wheel off a car. Perhaps he had never seen a boy at the top of my uncle's apple tree. I hid behind a branch.

Baschurch was very different from our village. It had so many shops: two butchers, two bakers, two grocers, two or more inns and garages with Benzol petrol pumps. There were large houses with grand names like The Firs, The Cedars and Boreatton Hall (a remand home — where the naughty boys went, Uncle said). Baschurch had a railway station; a church which was big brother to ours; and an earthwork larger and even more mysterious than ours, the Byrth. Baschurch people had interesting names like Dorricott, Muncaster, Heard, Druce, Onions and Bizell. Baschurch had a dame: Dame Agnes Hunt who founded the first orthopaedic hospital at Florence House.

From my vantage point I could not see the station, but I could hear a train drawing in. The release of steam, the snorts and whistles drew me down the tree; and, while the man had his back turned, I was through the hedge and down the road to the level-crossing gates.

The gates were open, the signals down. The train stood snorting on the track. Smoke billowed under an awning and blotted out the guard. He waited, waved his flag and ended the suspense. The release of steam, the savage blasts, the whistles all excited me. But I was not prepared for the sudden emission of smoke that then blacked out the scene.

67

I saw no more of that train than the last two carriages, rocking their way to Wales.

I wiped the spray off my face and puffed, still running on my toes, like a train, *pishoo-oo*, to my uncle's shop. The man at the garage dropped a spanner with a clang that added to the effect.

"You're puffing and blowing like a train," Aunt Mary said when I went in.

"You've been climbing trees again!" My mother pommelled my back. "And look at your seat!"

"Can't see my seat," I joked. But I could feel my ear.

Aunt Mary, with dignity and insight, beckoned us through to the back of the shop. "Something to see you on your way," she said. We thanked her as we stuffed our toffees out of sight.

Buoyed up, we trooped along the town-like street. Outside the butcher's shop we met our cousin, talking to her friends. One said she had some bantams to spare. Would we like them? I said please; and before my mother had time to protest a cardboard box was pressed into my arms. "Two dandies and a cock." I said my thanks and trotted on ahead.

We soon struck out across the fields: those riverside slopes that lustred in the early evening light. Tussocky with grass and clumped with rushes, they were alive with butterflies and birds: painted lady, peacock, partridge, peewit, pipit and snipe.

Krrrr-ic, a partridge showed the chestnut horseshoe on his breast, then dipped and scuttled with his cowering hen and all but disappeared. Then *ripriprip*, they rasped away on agitated, whirring wings; then

68

glided earthwards in an arc, like paper discs sent spinning from the hand.

John had found a meadow pipit's nest. He said he'd nearly trodden on it.

"Did you get an egg?" I asked.

"Just one." He showed it to me, wrapped up in his handkerchief: mottled brown and grey.

"A bit like a sparrow's," I said — because I hadn't got one, and sparrows laid so many eggs in the ivy on our house and they varied so much in colour I thought I could pass off one of them as a meadow pipit's, if it had a good label.

"See!" John replaced the egg in his pocket and grasped me by the upper arm, so hard I nearly dropped my bantam box. "A hare! Walk straight — it can't see us in front."

"It's a mole hill."

"No it's not. It's getting smaller, squatting down. Keep straight."

Up sprang the hare with large distended yellow eyes, and long extended yellow legs. And Belle and Laura found the leverets, blue-eyed, one, two, three, in couches in the grass at various points about the field.

"Leave them alone!" our mother yelled.

"Their parents will forsake them," shouted John in strong support.

"And where have you been?" Mother pounced and gripped him by the ear. His trousers bore the tell-tale, L-shaped, typical barbed-wire tear.

Later, in the sanctuary of the bedroom, John placed his meadow pipit's egg in his part of our collection, laid out lovingly on the marble-topped washstand in nests of moss and sheep's wool from the hedge. It looked like a model of the cobblestones. "Call note peet", the bird book said. "Pirated by cuckoos."

"Here, this will interest you," said John, one warm June night, rising up from a swamp of tropical bedclothes.

"'A little Wake was held at Ease Well, near the Perry stream not far from the Chapelry boundary.'" He was probing deeper into the parson's book. "'Until about 1863 this well was frequented by young people on Palm Sunday. The men indulged in a jumping contest, both high jump and long jump . . .'"

"I could have taken part in that," I boasted. "As you say, I leap like a mountain goat." It was the only thing at which I could just beat my brother. From frequent attempts to fly from sandstone walls around the farm I had developed a wonderful fluency in air.

"Just listen. 'The people partook of cakes and drank sugar and water —'"

"This must have been somewhere near the watercourse, not far from where we were the other day."

"Yes, but listen. 'Miss Burne in *Shropshire Folklore* relates that a clergyman who visited the scene in 1830 saw little boys scrambling for lumps of sugar which escaped from the glasses and floated down the brook which flows from the spring into the river'."

It was marvellous to picture the men from the fields stripped to their waistcoats, an extra piece of string to clip their trousers up, leaping a waggon rope stretched between two makeshift stands. Perhaps they long jumped over the stream, then used the rope again for a rousing tug-o'-war.

"There were fights as well", said John, "between the men of Ness and their neighbours from Ruyton-XI-Towns. 'The townsmen of Little Ness', it says, 'were taken to court for enclosing the lane, called Clemensyche, somewhere up the Ruyton road'."

I imagined the weavers in their dim-lit cottages startled at night by marauding bands of men from the Cliffe, breaking down fences and loosing out the cattle on the "lord's waste" by the lane. These men were more than shadowy figures from the past. They were the forefathers of Wat the Rat and Jack Birch from The Shruggs and Long John Evans from Rock Lane, near Nesscliffe Hill — famous for fighting in our day.

It was from one of these lanes under the hill that Pegleg Mumford came. She was an Amazon, aged fourteen. She had bulging legs, bouncing breasts, a long nose, short teeth and she smelt like a horse. In a word, she was strong. I lay awake concerned no more about contests between men from the past but about mine with her next day.

Once classes were over the following morning, I went home with the clear intention of not having any lunch and spending all my time practising the high jump in the little field at the back of the house. There I stuck two bean-poles in the ground and balanced a third on nails between.

"Coo-ee!" The call to lunch came earlier than expected and I weakened, having failed at what I thought was three-foot-six.

"What's the matter with you?" asked Mother, seeing me picking at my food.

"He's trying to keep his weight down for the sports," said Belle, who was wavyhaired, smiling and plump.

"Stuff and nonsense! You don't move from that table till you've finished the plate."

"Then you will be a crock," Laura whispered, and went on to sing "For the great day thyself prepare".

"Don't sing at the table," said Mother, upturning a basin and uncovering a pudding in a cloud of steam.

"What's that?" I asked with trembling voice.

"Spotted dick. It's rude to make remarks about the food."

"I didn't."

"No, but you were going to."

So, full of stew and spotted dick, I struggled back to school. It was more as lotus eaters than the well-tuned athletes of Ancient Greece that we approached the high jump that afternoon. After prayers we clanked our desk seats down and, the sun on our backs from the large hoppered windows now open to the south, we gave ourselves to books: *The Heroes*, *The Water Babies*, *Tom Brown's Schooldays* and the rest. Wild roses decked the window sills. Delicious languour lighted on us all. Even Hyler gave in. She neglected her fire. We read for hours, or so it seemed. Occasionally I took my eyes off the heroes — Perseus wrestling with Medusa,

72

Theseus with the Minotaur — to eye the real-life opposition in class.

There was Lofty Lloyd, solid and dull, in corduroy breeches and heavy boots. He couldn't run. There was Peggy Whiteside in a long white pinafore and Artie Griffiths half-asleep, in smelly cut-down wellingtons. ("You should not wear them all day long, they draw your feet." Miss Hyles knew that he had no proper shoes.) There was Big Fat Jelly Rump. And Dorothy, too ladylike to want her skirts to ride above her knees, Bobby Chesney who, less a pupil, more a monitor, was privileged to hold the rope and keep the score. There, too, was Pegleg Mumford, already wearing pumps, a short-sleeved shirt, short socks and a skirt that only barely covered her bottom.

"Right," said Miss Hyles. "High jump after play. Dorothy and Bobby will hold the rope." She did not add that she would bring her knitting out. We knew that anyway.

We jumped in the playground; the grass in the field was too rough. Bobby and Dot held the girls' long skipping rope between them. We started at only two foot, "to give everybody a go". All sixteen of us lined up by the wall. Girls, giggling, clutched their skirts and tripped into the rope like dolls. Heavy-breathing louts, brought into order now, were forced into mistakes at silly heights like two-foot-eight. At three foot there was only me and Pegleg left. Miss Hyles ended a row and, taking a tape measure, checked the height from the ground to the middle of the rope. "Good, that's correct." I knew that I could jump it straight. The "scissors" jumpers jumped it from the side and often at a higher point. I jumped it easily.

"Cleared it! By six inches!" Everybody cheered. But Pegleg cleared it too.

"Up one," said Hyler, checking it again. And so we went to three-foot-six. But now poor Dorothy complained of being tired. "My arm aches, Miss."

"Well, Billy, you can take the rope!" Not Big Fat Jelly Rump!

I felt the strength go from my legs. They checked the rope again. I jumped and as I did I swear the bully brought his hand up high. I touched the rope. That meant I had to jump again.

Then Pegleg jumped it clear. I tried again and failed.

"You've 'ad two goes," said Jelly Rump.

"I'll hold the rope with Bob," said Hyler.

"Teacher's pet," said some.

"No, fair is fair," said she. Winding her wool, she skewered the ball with the needles and thrust all in her woolly pouch. She took the rope. "Now check it, Dorothy! Quite perpendicular?"

"Yes, Miss."

I took my third attempt.

"You cleared it by six inches," cheered the crowd. And with them on my side, I struggled on to win. No thanks to gentle Dot or Big Fat Jelly Rump.

The end of June, and any day now the little Bamford cutter would fret its way through gilded seas of summer-scented hay. We tapped the glass to see if it would rain. It was "set fair". Hyler told me to take the two- and three-legged tadpoles which came in as spawn in March and tip them in the pit; and throw out the sticky buds, grown now to white attenuated palms in water that had begun to look and smell like stale cider in the jar. The fields beyond were wind-blown, scented with clover, trefoil and vetch. Our hearts were in the windrows now. After school, intoxicated with the scents and sudden flocks of company, we tossed and turned and tedded it and got it into cocks. We all helped each other. Men and boys came from all around and all pitched in with a will: the smiling Emrys, the rabbit catcher Wat the Rat, and Robin from Lancashire ("Aw reet, guv'n'r, 'ow's thisen? Fair t' middlin', middlin't fair? Well, what's t' do then? Oop on top?"). He always did the loading anyway. I rode on the horse-drawn rake, pulling it up when it was full and letting it down with a clang. We sweated and drank with the men — cider if not beer — swigging it from stone casks clad in wickerwork and drawing our arms over our mouths to show that we were men.

It was the tradition in the country for women and their children to take a week's holiday by the sea after their exertions in the hay harvest. The men would be content to take a little trip by pony trap to see how far advanced or otherwise their neighbours were. This tradition was resisted by attendance officers, of course — but teachers understood.

So, once our own hay was in the barn, Mother took us off to Rhyl. Charlie Parry brought his taxi up from Ruyton and took us and our trunks whose flapping labels all announced that we were going to stay with Mrs Jones, 61 West Parade, Rhyl, Flint.

No sooner were we all installed than we were scooped on to Baschurch station where the porter showed his style. He made me stare. Such fervour! Such attention! "Madam, if you please!"

"Come on, don't stand and stare! The train won't wait all day!" Mother hung on to her travelling hat and we were swept, it seemed, by a whirlwind into the carriage, all steam and smoke and fusty smells. "Communication cord. Penalty for improper use £5." Leather straps disappeared as windows rattled down, then appeared again as we drew them up. The engine heaved itself out of a huff into a cheerily chanted *chuffa-chuff-chuff*. A far cry from our pony trap!

We changed at Chester. Spindrift steam like rain blew on our faces, wild Welsh hills flew by; and then on widening nostrils fell the sharp salt smell of the sea. At no. 61, Mrs Jones, in all-Welsh black, height four-foot-six, her silver hair clamped in a tortoiseshell comb, smiled through her glasses and told us to make ourselves at home. "Mind how you go — don't run. D'you want to see the Jolly Boys? Oh, tea's at five, you won't want noise. It's quieter down here." She led us down another mile of carpets and banisters to where we would have tea.

Mother gave us free rein and five shillings for the week. I had to do better than last year when I spent my allowance the first day on a Services pocket watch and had to content myself with sitting and watching the second hand revolve minute by minute, ticking off eternity.

The sea, initially so magical to see and smell, was torture to the taste and touch. You went in sun-warmed and dry and exchanged a heaven of hot, inviting sand for a hell of thrashing, angry, stinging brine which left your feet cut, your ears pounding, your eyes sore, your skin sticky and raw with salt and sand. Dried off at last, you recognized in the pathetic face of a donkey a distant sympathy. "Only thruppence a ride," said the man with tarry teeth. But you knew that he would not let you go by yourself, and the donkeys only walked — it was a waste of money. What really attracted you to the donkey was the sadness in his eyes, the unfitness of those tiny feet to carry more than a child held on by its mother. Yet you knew that they could carry a man and one had carried God. The strength was all in the jaw with its matted, musky hair, quite soft to the cheek, and the stout, untouchable ears . . .

Then there was every shape and size of patterned stone and shell, smooth, ridged, convex or flat; seaweed straps like whips and driving reins and crackling sun-dried bladderwrack; sandcastles that were always built to stand against the tide — and never did. There was the terrifying Punch, the all-devouring crocodile and the little brown dog with the blue and white ruff who took no notice of it all. I did not put my penny in the box but meanly saved it for the Pierrots, after lunch.

"How much money've you got?" I asked my brother at lunch.

"Five-and-six," he said, incomprehensibly.

"Liar" was almost out of my mouth when Mother kicked my shin and ordered me to leave the table at once. "Your fingernails! Your hair!" I looked at my fingernails and, puzzled, found they smelt of donkey dust; much the same as they did when I rode Topsy. They were rimmed with mucky, tacky scurf.

"I took some bottles back," John added as we finished lunch; and left me standing speechless by a hat stand in the hall.

He took some bottles back? We hadn't had any bottles. Where'd 'e get them from? I turned the problem around in my mind, sea water working in my ears, as I sat in the front row of the pavilion waiting for the Pierrots to begin. The fiddlers scraped their fiddles, the dancers kicked their legs up high and the crazy clowns dropped their baggy trousers on the floor. "My pantaloons are on the floo-or," they cried repeatedly and everybody oohed and aahed, and the smart top-hatted man invited children on the stage.

"What's your name, son?"

"Peter," I said.

" 'Oh, Peter Piper picked a peck of pickled pepper; a peck of pickled pepper Peter Piper picked'. D'you know that? And what you goin' to be when you grow up?"

"A man," said I. The audience roared and I was quite enjoying myself. I was given a free ticket for the evening performance.

"I'm going to the Pierrots free tonight." I told my brother at tea.

"So what?" said he. "I'm going to the Wall of Death."

That night in bed he told me how two men on motor-bikes rode round and round the Wall of Death. They kept going higher and higher at right angles to a perpendicular wall. Something to do with centrifugal force, he said.

"Go on," said I.

"You'll see," said he.

"Then how much money've you got — still five-and-six?"

"Yes," said he, "I took some more bottles back. I've found a handy little shop that gives me a penny on a bottle — those with screw-on tops, they like. I'll show you in the morning. People leave their bottles everywhere. If you get round before the corporation clears them up you can get the money for them. See?"

With my new double-breasted security I sat smugly at the front of the pavilion for the Pierrots' matinees (half empty anyway), eagerly conforming with the compère's whims if he wanted to do a tongue-twister and ask me again what I was going to be. Mornings and evenings I relieved people of the burden of their empties. This way I was able to enjoy the terrifying Wall of Death, the Ghost Train, the bump-flashbump-and-trickle of the pin-table machines as the ball bearing tracked down to lose my hard-earned coins; and the bump-flash, *bump-bash* of the bumper cars . . .

The week flew by and soon, all sand washed out of our feet — but water oozing in my ears — we were approaching Baschurch station. Approaching! We'd passed it!

Mother pulled the communication cord. The train howled to a halt. Exchanges of words — "Taxi waiting . . . All these children . . ." "Tickets . . . A through train, ma'am, you know —" were tossed with the steam and smoke in the wind. "Right, madam. I'll get him to reverse, if you'll move along now to the rear of the train."

Lurching and lunging, we fell over our cases and picked ourselves up in time to be bundled out, covered in steam and smoke and embarrassment at the end of the platform.

"Five pounds' fine," muttered John. But Mother was waving amiably to the guard who could not now be seen for smoke.

And somehow we were home again; changed out of flimsy whites and floppy hats to coarse grey flannel shirts and cords. The corn had grown, the weeds had grown, the goslings had grown into geese. And Dad, who said he'd never been away, stayed in to hear the tale. What had kept him at home, and what welcomed us now with its most wholesome, comforting aroma, was the boiler full of home-brewed beer.

When I returned to Little Ness school on Monday morning for only one more week, Miss Hyles smiled and asked me if I felt the benefit. And during sums I smugly sucked the skin on my unsleeved arm, still tasting salty like the sea and feeling taut. I glowed. And Jimmy Roberts glowered.

That afternoon we leavers sat around like old contemptibles recalling deeds of glory from the past and wondering how to bring our time at school to a still more glorious end.

Visible through our large east window in the schoolroom was the little black figure of Mr Hulse behind the big drivewheel of the steam engine, spinning the small steering wheel (it seemed a dozen times) to turn the roller at the front an inch. The sun picked out the leaping horse in brass, the mascot of the Lancashire Road Roller Co. He had come to tar the road. He came with his wife and daughter nearly every year. I could see their van set up on the grass plot by the pit, an oblong, wooden, living-van with steps up to the door in front, a window at the side, a stovepipe peeping through the roof, all painted green, all spick and span. Outside, in shiny patent leather shoes, white ankle socks and a pretty frilly dress, was red-haired Gwendolene, picking clover in the grass.

"Lookin' at Gwendolene, are ya?" Jimmy sniffed.

"No."

"'Er unna come ta school, ya know."

"Not worth it now."

"Stop talking, you two," Hyler said. "For once!" She was putting away books. Neatly. In sets. In cupboards, and locking them up.

Gwendolene did not say books. She said boo — ks. She made it rhyme with flukes. I could not resist those double helpings of vowels coming from her little pink mouth. Gwendolene had amber eyes to go with her shoulder-length red hair and plucked at her socks with pretty white hands to show how fine they were. Her legs, I mean.

I had met her last year down the Valeswood road. Her father's van was parked in a lane that led to the marl pit where coots and moorhens made their nests. She asked me if I'd like a bit "o" look". I didn't know what she meant. Then she held up a four-leaf clover. "That's look," she said, and threaded the slender, pliant stem through a buttonhole in my shirt. It was then that I noticed her smell. It was the same as the scent of sun-warmed gorse which has in it a hint of milky coconut, the gentle spice of apricot. A summer smell, but cool and clean.

"Oh, luck!" I laughed and blushed.

She came with me to the marl pit. We saw a heron. "Oh, loo-k," she said, "a Jimmy langlegs!" We did not find a moorhen's nest close enough to the edge for me to reach an egg without taking my shoes and socks off. A thing I would not do in front of Gwendolene. We heard the *coo-coo*, and in the upturned root of a tree, we found the nest of a "stoompy-toddy" (Jenny wren). A ladybird lighted on my arm and Gwendolene charmed it into flight with:

> "Ladybird, ladybird, flyaway 'ome,
> Yor 'oos is on fyah
> An' yor cheeldr'n ah gawn;
> All except woon
> An' that's Sally Ann,
> She's curled oop oonder t'wawmin' pan."

The ladybird flared its wings and, like a tiny flame, it flew away.

She charmed me too, did Gwendolene. She introduced romance into nature. And "look". And the cool, clean smell of something not quite gorse and not quite apricot . . . "I love the smell of tar," said Jimmy into his sleeve.

I wish you'd roll in it, I thought, and then went back to dreaming.

After school that afternoon I helped Mr Hulse fill his water barrel from our pump.

"'Er drinks a lot o' watter, doos that 'oss," he said. I was bending down to pick up a bucket when the raised handle of the pump caught my eyebrow, hard on the bone. It came up like an egg.

"Ay, sorry, lad," said Mr Hulse. "Coom up to t'van. Missus'll 'appen 'ave the very thing for thee."

I peeped inside the van where Mrs Hulse, as pretty as a turtle dove, cooed around her model home. "Ay, lad, 'oo's fisted thee?" she said, and gave me a piece of homemade toffee.

"T'pump," I said, one swollen cheek to match my eye; and then, avoiding a head-on clash with Gwendolene, ran home for tea. I would probably have to milk.

The next afternoon, about half past five, there was the sound of hooves clattering on our cobblestones.

"It's Jack," said John.

"Which Jack?" my mother asked.

"From Dovaston."

"You mean Saint Martins, don't you? Clear the table, girls. I'll have to find him something to eat." And

83

in walked Jack. I didn't know whether to hide my face or not.

Jack was my Auntie Lottie's grown-up son; my idol in those days. Ramrod straight and groomed like a guardsman, Jack was said to have milked his cows the evening after his wedding still wearing his tails. He had a herd of Friesians now but he had started at his parents' home at Dovaston with one heifer calf. He now lived at St Martins, north of Oswestry. Tuesday was Shrewsbury's market day and he had called on his way home to see one of our in-calf cows.

I rushed outside to get the cows in. I was halfway through the milking when my brother came to help.

"You're quick," said he.

"Of course," said I. I was doing it to impress Jack. But why didn't *he* come?

The cows were turned out in the field when Jack and my father finished their tea. They were talking about the floods round Melverley in the spring. There, in the flood plain of the Severn, between Nesscliffe and the Breiddens, Jack, like many farmers, rented pasture for his stock. They talked of horses and cattle being stranded, neck-deep in water, and hay being carried out to them in boats. And there was a marvellous story of Uncle Eddowes, Jack's father, saying to Uncle Percy, who was only visiting him for lunch one Sunday: "Come on, Percy, we'll put those cattle up on higher ground." The river was rising at a record rate.

Off galloped Ragman, Eddowes's pony, with the two men in the float. They rounded up the cattle on to higher ground; but as they turned for home they found themselves cut off. The rising waters had left them directionless. Even the tops of the hedges had gone.

"Get home, Ragman!" cried Eddowes. And home went Ragman, half-swimming through the flood, the two men riding with their feet up in the float. "He knew the road, oright," said Jack. "Even when it wasn't there!"

We walked together, Jack and John and Dad and I, through fields where buttercups drank up the sun. Panhandled cuckoos called self-mockingly, careering round in crazed and crooked flight. Jack was admiring the state of our cattle, sleek and lustrous as they would ever be. He pulled elastic skin out from behind their bags and slapped their flanks.

"If a cow's doing well you can pull a handful of loose skin from her side," he said. "And you can tell a good stockman; the stock'll lick him all over. They wunna go near a bad un."

Jack smiled and jingled his money in his pocket, making me more than ever determined to emulate him.

For a moment he stopped jingling and the smile left his eyes. "Times are goin' to be bad, by the looks of things . . .", he said ". . . with all this talk about war."

My father shook his head. "I've seen it comin' a long time," he said. "Peace with bloody honour, my —" His coughing sent a shower of sparks from his cigarette and propelled the last word into the air. But it left a shadow on my mind.

"What'll you give fer 'er?" my father asked Jack, changing the subject and pointing to an in-calf, black and white.

Jack looked at her mouth. "Rising four," he estimated, "second calf."

"We call her Black Beauty," I said. Jack jingled away.

"Twenty-eight pounds," I volunteered.

"Well, you're not a bad judge," Jack said, and added: "Your father should give you the calf."

We stood between the strawberry-coloured Kelsall cow and the brindled Alice, Jack and Dad and John and I stroking each with either hand. They were older than I was. They had come with us from the Wigmarsh.

Your father should give you the calf — I'll keep him to that, I thought. I hoped it would be a heifer. Then, when it was as old as Alice, I would be as old, and as rich, as Jack.

CHAPTER
THREE

Harvest and Holidays

My eye went down. "It inna even black," said Jimmy disappointedly, next day. I would have liked it to have been multi-coloured, as a true badge of honour.

Mornings of the last few days at school were spent making sure we knew the Ten Commandments — that we would not covet our neighbour's wife — and all those tablets of a different kind: length, capacity, square measure, weight; how many rods there were in an acre and how many gallons in a peck. In the afternoons, Miss Hyles, knowing our mounting interest in the harvest fields, allowed us boys extra time to finish our village books. The girls, her "little assistants", popped everything else away, while she sat like Britannia, minus her trident, with only Jimmy's babble, a last ripple, breaking at her feet, before the tide went out.

The last day came.

"They're cuttin' the Vipers Hills t'day," hissed Jimmy in my ear.

"No?"

"Yes. Silas was scythin' the 'adlands 'smorning. They'll finish it 'safternoon."

"I'll see you 'sevenin'," I said and, newly inspired, got on with my book.

"*Tow-row-row*, the rabbits run . . ." My pages were littered with rabbits spurting up and spilling over the sheaves. They never stood a chance. Wherever they ran there were hundreds of obstacles scattered by the champing, chattering, whirling sailbinder. Sometimes it simply cut their legs off, no hopers from the start.

Proud of my efforts, I took them up to show Miss Hyles. She wondered how I drew my rabbits somersaulting over sheaves.

"Like planes, Miss."

"What? Like aeroplanes, you mean?"

"Yes, Miss. I turn the paper upside down." I showed her. I drew the rabbit the right way up, then turned the paper round again. "Now the rabbit's upside down."

"Simple," she said, "the idea, I mean," and went on with her knitting.

The clock ticked on.

"We've missed our play," said Jimmy, who had done no work.

Then Hyler rose. "Stop now," she said, "but keep your village books. Our world is changing fast, you know. Lighten our darkness . . ."

"It's only three o'clock," Jimmy announced as we reached "all perils of this night . . ."

Stunned by this concession, we left the silent classroom silently: the blackboard shiny wet and clean, the books all packed away, the windows closed, the window pole in place, the old piano dumb. Even BFJR, who had never been known to leave the cloakroom without aiming his bag at somebody's back, was strangely muted now. He hung his head, looked somewhat small, and smiled a rueful smile.

But with the smell of hot tar in our nostrils, the crackle and crunch of the roller and the fusillade of chippings in our ears, the dancing atmosphere before our eyes, we left the unreal world of school behind. And yonder lay the fields, beckoning, white, all ready to harvest: those fields that were never so alive, though there was death in every movement of the knife.

I did my jobs at home and, after tea, I headed for the Vipers Hills.

Till now a sea of near-white, tassel-headed oats, it was usually the first field in our area to be cut, and was only a stone's throw past the school. Silas, the general handyman, had scythed round the headlands, and the binder, after working all morning and afternoon, had reduced the standing crop to that fateful triangle from which the hopeless rabbits had to run. The man on the binder waved an arm and shouted "Fox!" Perhaps it was a hare.

"No," said Jimmy Know-all, "never a 'are in 'ere."

"Nor rabbits either, if it's true there is a fox," said John, just home from school and holding on to Gyp, his whippet.

A squeal announced that Bob had clubbed one with his stick. "There's one for Ganker's rabbit pie." He spat, and spliced the rabbit's legs and hoicked him on his stick.

"No, put him under a shauve," said John, "or they might take him off you at the end."

"*Ja wohl*," said Bob, who spattered his conversation with bits of his dad's 1918 German mixed with *hasta la vistas* and vamooses from the Spanish civil war.

We beat around the edges of the dwindling triangle with our sticks. "Keep out of the corn," shouted the men. "Stand back, and let the dog see the rabbit!" But we were eager for a sight of anything ourselves: a hare, a fox, a rat, a weasel or a stoat.

"*Tow-row-row . . .*" Accelerating now, the rabbits started to run in all directions. We ran and tripped; they ran and tripped; we lost our sticks, they lost their legs. We nearly lost our heads.

Gyp scooped up rabbits out of the air, sent hurtling by their own momentum off the sheaves. And then he saw the hare, racing from a corner uphill on a clear diagonal, uninterrupted by sheaves, which would lead him to the Ruyton road and on to open fields. "'E'll never ketch 'im, John," we said. But John had gone, his ears up like the hare's, leaving the cotton-tails to us. If there was a fox we never saw him; and all I got was one old milky doe.

As we left the gate of the Vipers Hills we saw the dark silhouette of the coppice blackened by a thunder cloud. "It always rains when they cut the Vipers Hills," we said in unison.

"And I'll bet that fox is safe inside that wood," said Bob.

"Or in our 'en 'ouse, very like," said I. I dropped my milky doe by the gate and ran to shut the front-field henhouse up. I should have looked inside, I thought, but turned and ran for home. My legs were scratched, my feet and ankles skewered with the stubble of the corn. A chilling numbness gripped my heart. I panted, "Bear me well, brave sandals, for the hounds of hell are at my heels."

There at the gate was John, Gyp and the hare. "Gyp caught him on the open grass," he said. "That's harder than on the stubble. What you got? A milky doe. I'll have it for my ferrets, yes?"

Jimmy Roberts lived at the foot of the Cliffe. His house backed on to the rock, a kind of sandstone bookend which had parted company from all the books tumbled about on the shelves and ledges beyond.

His father was a roadman, spectacled and quiet as a medieval history don. He carried his light mac folded neatly over his shoulder and secured somehow, so that in mounting and dismounting his fully appointed motor-bike it was not dislodged.

He was a most controlled mover. I had seen him wheel his motor-bike down his field-sized garden, through the gateway, the spongy suspension softening the drop into the road, start the bike purring like a big cat and glide into the sandstone hollows of Hopton, tuned to the harmony of the universe.

Inside the house, Jimmy's fiery mum, with a head like a thornbush and eyes like live coals, used to sing like a versatile nanny-goat. "Juanita", "La Paloma" — opera if you like! Always cooking, always singing in her comfortable, carefree, cavernous house. Horse hair sprouted out of the genuine leather chairs. Wood burned in the genuine cast-iron grate. Genuine Spode.

Genuine brass. Copper. Cabinets. Ornaments. Pictures. And the genuine smell of battered fish.

And Jimmy, well, he was always challenging me to to something: jumping gorse bushes, dropping off high ledges, walking along five-barred gates, holding my breath in a bucket of water or climbing a tree like a telegraph pole . . .

The first week of that long summer holiday he really tested me. "There's a kestrel's nest up there," he said, pointing high into a pine tree on the Valeswood road. "I been watchin' 'er go in that 'ole." It was not so much a hole as a hollow between two fangs. There were no low branches, so there were no handholds; no handholds, no footholds. For fifteen feet or more.

I decided that if I could get a rope over a branch, about twenty feet up, I might have a chance. I was lighter than Jimmy who, for all his bravado, was a bit stocky for this job. It was close to a field being cut that afternoon, but only just begun. We didn't want to be seen, so we decided to leave it till eight o'clock, when we judged the men would have stopped for the night.

Armed with a "wantin" or waggon rope, I began the assault before eight, and before Jimmy arrived. I slung the rope over the arm-branch twice so that it would be less likely to slip, and knotted it as high over my head as I could reach. I had my foot burning in the foothold thus provided and was trying to stop it spinning when Jimmy rode up on his bike.

"Watcha!"

"Hold on, Jim! Can you steady the bottom a bit?"

I realized now that there was about twelve feet of rope unknotted and bucketing around, now lurching too near the trunk, now too far away. I couldn't draw the two sides of the rope together. If I hauled with two hands on one side it slipped round the branch. If I tried to use my feet on the trunk the rope swung me away. Heaving myself up, in free air as it were, with only the rope to purchase on with my legs, was so punishing to my arms I thought I should be sick. Flakes of pine bark came down like shrapnel off the branch above and I couldn't look up without getting some in my eyes. When I did get up, the rope had worked itself too close to the trunk for me to swing my body over. Jimmy stood on the knot halfway up the rope and helped to steady it, making it just possible for me to get my body prone along the branch.

Then the flak from the kestrels came down. At this time of night they were both on the nest. I got a good foothold on a burl and could reach the hollow where the nest was if I could only see what I was doing. When I looked up, scales of bark descended in my eyes. Branches like spurs stuck out at right angles to the trunk. They jabbed my ears. I had to grope blindly till I felt the eggs. One — two — three — four.

"I'll take only one."

"Whatcha mean? What about me?"

"There are only four." I should have said three.

"That's all right, 'er'll lay s'more. They 'ave up to six or seven."

"Not often."

"'Urry up! It'll be dark!"

All right for him, I thought. I was working in the dark anyway.

I got two eggs in my pocket, warm and hard and round as stones.

The descent was easy. I scratched my ear and burnt my hands and the insides of my legs. Warm blood bubbled in my ear and congealed with my sweat. I felt as if I'd scaled the battlements of a castle. "A kestrel's nest is a fortress."

"F— fortress. Where's the egg?" One was damaged. "I found it. I told you where it was!" Jimmy was going to have his rights. So I kept the damaged one, the only one in my collection of fifty-five eggs not in perfect condition.

A few days later I was up on the Cliffe with Jimmy, again looking for nests. We ranged around the quarry and the sullen plantations of spruce and larch. We shouldered our way through the bracken where Jimmy built his dens. And we screwed our eyes up at a stricken old oak tree — a likely place, he said, to find a tawny owl's nest.

He knew all the best places to find owls' nests. They gave themselves away, he said, by their pellets on the ground: the screech owls round the quarry; the longeared in the conifer woods where they sometimes used an old crow's nest; the tawny owl, well, he was like the white owl, he built in rocks or trees or sometimes in a rabbit hole. Some owls, like sparrow hawks and kestrels, sometimes used an old magpie's nest. But he'd never found a tawny owl's. "It's got to be in a 'ole," he said.

I was used to putting my hands in holes. There was always a fear that something might sink its teeth into your fingers. A thousand nerve endings super-charged by imagination were brought into play. High up, it might be an owlet with a beak like nail scissors. Low down, it might be a rabbit hole taken over by a fox. My one and a half fingers had inserted themselves into a long-tailed tit's nest and snuggled in the moss of a wren's. My mother said I couldn't keep my fingers out of things . . .

Jimmy Roberts had an epidermis like an armadillo. His skin was ruckled round his joints like a pig's. He could slide his hand along a troughing to get a ball, which I never liked to do. Or put his whole arm down a drain.

"Put your hand in there," he said, pointing to a hole in a tree. It was above my head. "Go on, it wunna 'urtcha!"

"What is it?"

"You'll see."

I could just reach by stretching to the limit. It felt like a disturbance of air, the draught around the edges of cards super-shuffled, the wind playing with paper, the furriness softening into wax. I brought my hand out smartly. "You rotten sod!"

"Go on, lick it!" I licked my middle finger, smeared with a liquid gleam of sweet, sticky honey.

"Go on, have some more."

He was up there in a trice, scooping it out and pulling out pieces of the comb — fragments of flaked wax like solid olive oil, but far more tasty.

"Look out!" The bees were on the attack. Every one power-diving me. I ran, my arms flailing, my shirt flapping, bees in my hair, under my collar. Perhaps in my ears. I made sure I kept my mouth shut. I shook them out of my shirt. I rolled in the bracken. Hot nails were being driven into my neck and the undersides of my arms. A cloud came over my eye. An awning of puffed-out flesh. My ear throbbed. I felt scalded all over.

I ran and ran, insensate. Who saw me I knew not. Who heard me I cared not. But my mother heard me a mile off and had the blue bag of starch ready. Who saw me after saw a blue moonface, eyeless as a giant puffball. The Invisible Man!

"And the poor bees die," said my mother.

"You should have used bicarb," said Belle. "Bicarb for bees. Vinegar for wasps!"

Halfway through the holidays Audrey came to stay. She often came, in summer, riding bareback, bumpety-bump, on her little brown pony Bonny from Osmarston. Summer was the time for escapades. And Audrey was the person to promote them.

Audrey was our cousin. She had permanent blue, far-seeing eyes. She was quick. For instance, I could never understand how she could get up sometimes after me and be washed and dressed while I was still struggling into my shirt, the wrong side out. "Put your clothes in the right order when you go to bed" was her simple advice. But how did she get that shine on her early-morning face? "Soap," she said. "I rub it on! And then I wash in the rain tub and put my water wave in where I can see it in the window." She made me take more of a pride in myself. And how she worked! Audrey could milk two cows while I milked one. She had the fire lit in the morning and the kettle boiling and the breakfast laid — all much to Mother's satisfaction.

Mother approved of Audrey. She was "brisk and businesslike". She did not "gawp". She did not let the grass grow under her feet. She was, indeed, an unexploded packet of gumption, elbow grease and what our mother embarrassingly called "spunk". And, as a result of Audrey's efficiency, we had more time for adventure . . .

"You mustn't bathe too soon after lunch," said Mother when Audrey suggested we go down to the river one afternoon.

"We won't, Auntie May," said Audrey. "We'll spend time in the fields." Spending time in the fields meant rolling down the Banky Meadow and making ourselves sick.

"We'll take the ponies," she said. "It's too hot to walk."

"You can't all ride on two small ponies," Mother said.

"I'm not going," said John.

"Why not?" asked Mother.

"Girls," said he, inexplicably looking at me.

We ran our dinners down catching those two ponies in the field. Bonny was dumpy, docile and dull. Topsy was up on her toes and showing off. She arched her neck and arched her flying tail. At last we cornered her, still snorting at the front and back.

"She'll cool off in the river," I said.

"You don't take her in?" said Audrey.

"I do," said I.

"Don't forget your costumes," called Mother from the house. She ran down the little yard with a bundle of towels and costumes wrapped inside. "And mind you close the gates" was her last, despairing cry.

So Belle and Laura, Audrey and I set off with our ill-matched steeds through the village. Belle and Laura were all right on Bonny; but I could not hold Topsy in — or Audrey on. She landed in a laughing heap. We decided it would be better for one to ride and one to walk. We would all take turns. Past Little Ness House decorum prevailed. But when a man shouted from the stackyard at Home Farm "Get off and milk it!" Audrey was convulsed. Ganker Yeomans who lived next door to the Chesneys came, bow-legged, to the gate to see what all the noise was about.

"Sh!" I said, restoring order in the ranks.

"Bobby and Vic have gone down already," the old lady said. "Too soon after their dinner, you know!"

I did not know how to react. I was not really in the Chesneys' circle; those brighteyed, wild, freewheeling Celts. They moved in an orbit of their own which often included my daring brother John; but I was a hanger-on, and justly punished sometimes for my pains. Five years ahead of us, they had long since graduated from capering on the crossroads or cutting a dash on the Cliffe. While we rode ponies they perfected their incredible balancing acts on bikes. They rode backwards, sitting on their upturned handlebars. They could rear up in the air. They could ride on one wheel. And they were so fit themselves that down at the river they could jack-knife and swallow-dive out of trees. They could take themselves apart and reassemble their own bodies as they did their bikes, piece by double-jointed piece.

"I don't care if I don't bathe today," I announced, as it happened, to myself. Belle and Laura with Bonny were by now out of sight. Audrey, after dismounting and suddenly vaulting a five-barred gate, was wrestling with a sheep in the field. I was still standing with my mouth open when she returned.

"Presence of mind," she said, "that's what you need! When you see a sheep on its back you roll it over. Otherwise it'll die!" Her eyes blazed periwinkle blue. "Ride on," she said. "In majesty!"

We travelled on, not worried about time; not worried really whether we bathed. Adcote was a paradise at any time. A branch of the Birchall family lived there then: Fred, Mrs Fred, Maureen, Meraud and Elwin her twin. They lived in a ramble of roses, a gloom of hatches and a twitter of loose, worm-eaten planks. Laughter and water ran through the house. You stepped out of the kitchen almost on to the mill-wheel, undershot with climbable paddles — a marvellous place for Hide and Seek. Ducks dabbled everywhere: Khaki Campbells,

Indian runners (comically pivoting on their tails), Muscovies and Aylesburys, alongside Chinese and Emden and Toulouse geese. They traipsed across the bridge. They turned the mill pond cloudy grey and left their curly, parti-coloured feathers everywhere. Upstream, where the river had been diverted, there were eel traps and a waterfall under which we would stand, after bathing in the sandy shallows higher up, in a dry arc of peace.

"They're all at the waterfall," Mrs Fred sang from an upstairs window.

"Thanks," we called, and trotted and skipped across the field. Everyone was there: the Chesneys and the Millingtons, the Birchalls and the Griffithses. The Chesney boys ran after the girls and flicked towels at them. They could make a towel crack like a horsewhip. Crack! The girls giggled and screamed and ran squawking and spluttering into the water. Patient Bonny was unmoved. But Topsy could not be left tied to a gate with a shindy like that going on.

"Take her in," said Audrey. The spare costume Mother had provided for her did not fit. It must have belonged to one of our cousins from the time when boys' costumes hung down to the knees and climbed up over the shoulders and covered the chest.

"Long johns," I said and Audrey laughed. "Come on, I'll haul you up behind." So, with a click of the tongue, we sailed off down the river aboard our foam-white ship. Topsy took to the water with ease, her bold head riding high, her nostrils flared, those active legs striding the water trail and her everlasting tail unfolding in her wake.

Suddenly I realized that Audrey's struggling arms had gone from round my waist. She was in the water. She was shouting, "I can't swim! I can't swim!" Topsy was going with the current. I hollered, "Hang on to her tail!" My sisters were yelling, "The waterfall! The waterfall!"

I pulled hard on the reins to steer the pony to the right-hand side. There were only certain places where she could mount the bank to get out. We found one just in time, before the river shot off to the waterfall, or went on almost currentless where barbed wire and the eel traps would have barred our path.

Topsy thrust herself up the bank and I, dismounting smartly, slipped the bridle off before she shook herself till she rattled, water spurting everywhere, and then rolled over several times.

I left her grazing contentedly and went in search of my shipwrecked crew.

But I needn't have worried. Presence of Mind was saved. A watchful Millington, perched in an alder overhead, dived out of the tree and dragged the gulping, laughing Audrey to the bank, her long johns spouting water from their seams.

Smelling of river — a scent as sweet as cowflop, and as flat — we straggled home across the fields. Topsy had somehow lost a shoe. We could not ride her on the road. Belle, Laura and Bonny again went ahead. Audrey was intent on something in a hedge. "Who's been pogging here?" she called.

"What d'you mean, pogging?" I asked.

"Pulling out nests," she explained.

"Magpies, I expect," I yawned, but went to take a closer look. And there, in a thicket of bramble mixed with hawthorn and sloe, was the unmistakable nest of a long-tailed tit. It was unmistakable because of the hundreds of feathers scattered about, with pieces of lichen, moss, sheep's wool, horse hair — even the silken filaments of spiders' webs. Misshapen though it was, it looked like the little woolly hat of a doll. Carefully I tried to turn it to reveal the hole which is normally in the upper half of the front of the nest. Where only one finger would have seemed too big before, there was space enough now for two. I felt inside. It was snug but cold.

"Any left?" asked Audrey, her eyes like cornflowers now.

"Just one." I said. "Have you got one?" But Audrey wasn't there: presence of mind had sent her to a nearby barbed-wire fence to fetch a piece of wool. "Wrap it in this," she said. "I don't save eggs. Just sheep."

It was such a plain little thing, the egg. One of a possible clutch of ten, fifteen or even more. I thought of it as an orphan which I could not save from death; but I could save it from destruction. As I folded the wool round it I was fearful that the wind might blow it away.

"You're trembling," Audrey said, as she wrapped our costumes and towels together, and, taking control of Topsy as well, she left me free to carry the egg, two-handed, home. Yes, it was plain; it was tiny. But it was treasure. And it caused my heart to sing.

★ ★ ★

After some weeks running wild I thought it was time to sit down and consider. Work, I reasoned, might be more profitable than play. The Vipers Hills' oats were already in the barn. Barley and wheat were being lugged. There rolled the waggons, shires sure-footed in the shafts. "Owd fast! Owd 'ard!" the cries went up. The load moved on. Then stopped. The kitchen maids appeared with baskets spread with redlined linen cloths. The men ate greedily. Then gulped and swigged their beer from big stone jars. I hung about till someone said, "The little lad can lead the horse!" I came of age.

When Gyp and John came home from deepest Startlewood with lolling tongues and triumph in their eyes, I countered all John's claims.

"I led the horse!" I said.

"So what? I helped to load," said he.

I told him how I liked to feel the horse's warm breath on my hand, and smell it sweet; and how I'd shout "Owd fast! Owd 'ard!" And how, if I forgot, the loader shouted back — if he was still on top.

I didn't tell about the language I had heard, the underhanded sniggers, the sudden set-tos there had been, and crude attempts to pick a fight.

"And then they put the wantins on, hitch up the chain horse: 'Hold yer up!' and off we go. 'Whoa, steady now.' Wheels, harness, ropes all creaking to the barn."

"I know," said John. "And nobody gave you anything, and you never got your tea." I wondered how he got his tea. It must be that he takes his dog, I

103

thought. No man could sit and eat his bait and not give Gyp a bite . . .

The nights were drawing in; the yellow moon grew larger than the sun. We started to use the hurricane lamp around the cowhouses at night. Life, which had gone giddy for a time, rolled back into a tighter gear. Earnestness and purpose returned to the fold with the onrush of the ripening fruit. We could not strip the trees of their plums and apples fast enough. And pears dropped on the cobbles of the little yard. Geese gobbled them. Half-swallowed, they protruded from their necks. When a dealer brought his lorry crammed with crates and offered us a pound a strike for damsons we really thought we would be rich. He left some crates, but not enough. A strike was ninety pounds. A man could pick one in a day.

The bark of damson trees secretes a warm and bubbly gum like frankincense. The dusky ruby drupes taste more like myrrh. They paralyse the tongue. When black and ripe they make you sick.

"The dealers don't eat them," said John, who was beyond temptation. "They want them for dyeing."

"They'll die," I wretchedly agreed. The thorny branches scratched my arms and ribs; itchy twigs and scales of bark settled in runnels of sweat round my waist. Grit dropped in my eyes. "A pound a strike," I murmured, sweating on.

So harvest was not over yet; but the fun most certainly was. John and I picked for days. We filled the crates, we filled the bath, we filled our mother's clothes baskets with plums. Out of the top of a damson tree we would see, in the evening, the hens in the front field gather round the door of the henhouse, taking turns to go to bed. In the fields beyond the Cow Lane, lines between the stubble would have turned from gold to green where clover had grown up. Those fields, lately so full of folk and bristling with energy, would be empty now except for a scattering of hens still pecking hopefully for some remnants of shed grain.

When bath and crates and baskets had been filled we'd have to wait for the dealer to come and, with his light-weight money, pay us out. It went on clothes for school. We eyed our empty bins, we eyed our half-picked damson trees.

Suddenly, while resting on a five-barred gate, the silence would be shattered by a Spitfire from Tern Hill, flying at us straight out of the trees. "Ya nearly 'ad me yed off!" John would cry and wave his arm impotently, and I would run to see if Topsy was all right. It was the end of the aboriginal dreamtime. And summer wasn't summer any more.

CHAPTER
FOUR

War — and a Taste of Town Life

War was declared on 3 September 1939. The next day I found myself in uniform battling with an unready bicycle to Montford Bridge, then travelling at high speed towards Shrewsbury in an overcrowded bus. The bus dropped us by a tannery that smelt of death. There was a sweet shop on the corner kept by a man with one dead, misdirected eye. There were slums — the sunless slums of Priory Road. I was glad to get to school to have a drink. But the water from the zinc cup chained to a conduit tasted dead. Everything about this part of Shrewsbury seemed dead and tannin brown. The street urchins held up at the half-doors of dark brown tenements opposite the tannery sucked dark brown toffeed fingers with their dark brown toffeed teeth. Their slatternly mothers had toffee on their aprons and toffee in their hair. The lunch was dark brown stew and I sat through a dark brown afternoon.

Our form master was a foxy little man who did not wear a gown. He lived, someone said, in Leebotwood or Smethcott in the direction of Church Stretton and kept pigs. His crumpled corduroy suit was crusted with dry curds of meal. He was all ginger and brown; his hands were stained with nicotine, so too was his moustache. He had a sharp blue-eye, a quick acerbic manner and a fizzy gait that made you think of ginger beer. His collar was unironed, his boots thick-soled and tagged and brown. You noticed things about his back — his coat worn thin, his stringy hair — from his habit of disappearing into the paint room where, someone also said, he kept his tots among the pots ... For, unconventional as he was, Whisky Johnny (as everyone called him) was an artist. He taught art to the whole school and, as our form master, ministered to our elementary needs. Like English and maths.

The art room was lofty, cluttered and comfortable: an inaccessible repository for easels, unfinished portraits, landscapes, still-lifes and dust-collecting plaster casts. It was, in fact, the best-dressed room in the school — the only freely decorated one. Whisky Johnny made it look lived in, just like his clothes. It was home for himself and us.

To get so many Davieses and Joneses seated alphabetically; to dole out books (which had to be covered at home); to talk about the rules that had to be obeyed — where we could go and where we could not go, for there were areas given up to girls; to see that timetables, ruled wrongly first and done again, were properly filled in; these matters all took time. And then Whisky Johnny had to explain the school motto: *Possunt Quia Posse Videntur* — "You heard what the headmaster said it meant: They can because they think they can. It does not mean *you* can because you think *you* can. Did I hear someone speak?"

"What's *Porta Latina*, sir?"

"The gateway to Latin." He gave a sniff and issued more books: Marten and Carter's *History*, Durrell and Fawdrey's *Geometry*, Florian's *First French Course* . . .

"And now we've got that sorted out, my name's Maltby — Mr Maltby, if you please."

He gave out still more books: Selections from "Q" (Sir Arthur Quiller Couch), *A Tale of Two Cities* and *Kidnapped*. "See how much you can read now," he said. Poor old Q! I think we all chose *Kidnapped*, hoping for adventures of the Treasure Island kind, for all the gloomy opening, the "naethings" and the "dinnae ye kens".

While we were journeying with David Balfour to the House of Shaws, Mr Maltby passed between the rows of desks, muttering for no apparent reason: "Was he pushed or did he fall?"

That first day I fell. And I was pushed.

In the mid-morning playtime I nearly escaped the traditional dumping in the Dungeon by running head-down like a pig between breeches. The Dungeon was a steep-stepped exit (locked) at the bottom of the playground on to the riverside walk surmounted by heavy iron railings (spiked) from which the senior boys spat on newcomers incarcerated below. Escape was harder the longer you survived and the handling extra rough.

I managed to find the toilet by the end of playtime. Head boy Herdwick stood like a horse lazily loosing out his thing, his nose high-arched and ridged at the top. Big nose, big thing, I thought, and dribbled back to lessons up unending steps.

"Here comes the Big Mess from Little Ness," cracked Whisky Johnny, setting off a roar of beefy laughter. I tried to slide unnoticed into my seat, open Durrell and Fawdrey's *Geometry* and fathom out the size of L ABC. I could find A, B and C on the diagram; but where was L? (I was to spend a whole term trying to get an angle on geometry.)

Most of the afternoon, in contrast to the hectic morning, I spent terror-struck by the passage in *Kidnapped* where Davie mounts the steps to the tower in the dark and nearly falls to his death. We checked our gas masks, listened to instructions on air-raid precautions and cheered when the headmaster told us that we should in future only come to school in the morning. Groans followed his announcement that that meant Saturday as well. A school from Liverpool would occupy the building in the afternoon.

For the remainder of that first week we took sandwiches for lunch. Even if we managed to catch the one o'clock bus out of Shrewsbury we would still be late home. We tried, not very successfully, doing our homework at school. On the Wednesday afternoon I went to the pictures. On Thursday I went to the baths. I had seen Johnny Weissmuller as Tarzan swimming for endless minutes under water. At the baths I tried to do the same. I surfaced feeling sick: nose, ears, eyes all smarting with the chlorinated water and the grey-green, closed-up air. I looked up at the high balcony rail from which John and some older boys were diving into the six-foot end. Above the balcony was a clock. Above the clock, a ledge. My head ached. The noise in those old Shrewsbury baths was such that you could hear it across the road in school.

I could understand now why John was never bullied. He was such a daredevil, in a very quiet way. Everyone was shouting, "Off the clock, John! Dive off the clock!"

If anyone could do it, John could. He dived out of trees into the river at home. He was as skinny as a swallow. He had no nerves. I supposed too he was the best climber there. He could climb a telegraph pole. Almost.

I looked again. The pool was hushed and everyone was still. Only John moved, inching his way from the balcony to a bracket, from the bracket to a beam, from the beam to the board that was the ledge above the clock. And then he dived. I thought he would never come up . . .

On the way home John, two or three other lads and I stopped by a hedge to settle the question which of us, if any, could smoke a cigarette inside a minute. Watches checked, a match was struck and we puffed away till sickness overcame us one by one. But I was the last to go down. I hadn't inhaled.

Late home, Mother declared that she couldn't dry any more things, that the hens all needed cleaning out and if we had nothing better to do we could put salt between the cobblestones.

★ ★ ★

"Dukes," said Whisky Johnny at school on Friday, "if I forget to set homework, you're the monitor responsible for reminding me."

Dukes was the one who gave out books, opened windows and held the door open for the master going out with an armful of *National Geographics* which had occupied us while he thought of the next lesson. He had an elder brother who was a prefect and Dukes was going the same way. Nice lad. But you wouldn't catch the rest of class 2B leaping to oblige.

"What shall we do tonight then, sir?" Dukes piped from his prompt box near at hand.

"Let's see," said Johnny, fingering his beard. "Write about an ordinary man; just someone you happen to know, not a well-known figure but someone who might be — in a quiet way — a bit of a hero!" He wrote the title in capital letters on the blackboard and left us to think about it: AN ORDINARY MAN.

I was still thinking about it, salting round the cobblestones that evening after tea. John was already doing his homework. Laura and Belle were helping me. "Where did all these cobblestones come from?" Laura asked.

"Telford's rejects," I replied. "Too big to go in an Irish navvy's mouth!" Mother called them the stones that cried out.

The milkman trundled large twelve-gallon churns across those cobblestones. I tried to emulate his single-handed virtuosity. It was easy to twirl the lid with two hands; you just hoped the lid would stay on. But Ginger could rotate a full churn with his index finger

111

casually pressed on the centre of the lid. Then throw it up on the lorry as if it were a tin of Vim.

Corn merchants backed in. Coal merchants backed out. And the hauliers drove the staring cattle up their slatted ramps. Milk oozed from the milch cows' teats. And Davy Vow, a quick-witted little man with a billowing smock, would rope the porker, petted till he weighed two-hundred weight, and lay him out expiring on those stones. It was for such a pig that Dad had ordered so much salt.

The butcher, the baker, the egg man, the oil man, all jingling leather money bags, all clanked the iron gate. My favourite was Norman, the oil man, with his tilted, shiny hat and clear blue, candid eye. His order taken at the door, we would jingle back to the covered waggon, an Aladdin's store of oil lamps, candles, mops and brooms, of scrubbing brushes and black lead, of soaps and waxes, polishes, dusters, bootlaces and string. The tanks had taps of brass and there was every kind of funnel for the foaming, gushing, fuming paraffin.

I would help him with the haul: a couple of tins of paraffin, a new yard broom, a dozen candles and two hundred cigarettes for Dad. Norman, sucking air through his strong clean teeth, dimpling one cheek, blowing out the other, with a twitch of one ear and a wink, sometimes gave me a threepenny bit.

I would put it with my secret hoard in the bing, the place where hay was stored ready to be pushed through a space into the cows' mangers. At the bottom of the fresh-cut wads was a mattress of old hay permanently left to moulder and nearly resembling muck. All

112

through the winter the bing was the favourite sleeping place of William the tramp. William "the Silent" Mother called him. Bushy-bearded and sad-eyed, he had long fingers and a kind of faded elegance which made him an acceptable tramp. My threepenny bits were never disturbed. But then one day, to my delight, I found a sixpenny piece had been added to my hoard. I did not move them again but left them, like a clutch of eggs, to grow.

"You dreaming, or something?" asked Belle. "You'd better get the cows in, hadn't you?" The cows were standing by the gate, waiting to come in. We did not milk till late.

"I'll do my homework first," I said and rushed indoors. "I won't be long." I suddenly realized that the man I should write about was the one who had been missing from my thoughts.

I wrote down all I knew about my father's gallantry in the war; how he won the Military Medal by going alone into a wood occupied by three hundred Germans to bring out his wounded companions. At some point they had crossed the Somme, those men, hanging on to their horses' tails.

I could not tell it all.

"Go and get Scott in off the road," my mother called from another room. "He'll get run over!" Poor old Scott, he'd been going to get run over for years. He was our old sheep dog; he was older than any of us. Older even than the cat, or Alice the Wigmarsh cow. He was stiff in his hind legs and his sunny old eyes had grown dim behind clouds. He was lying there in the middle of the road, sun-warmed and spread with the first leaves to fall from the conker trees. He would lie there till after dark, if we let him. "Come on, old soldier," I said, tugging him into the house.

"Tell them about the bully-beef tin!" Mother called out, as I sat down to my homework again. "The one that blew up on the stove, and went all over the roof of the trench!"

That was only one of the stories my father told, sitting on the stone outside the gate, his cap tilted up, the fire rekindled in his eyes.

"What was the general doing," he'd ask, "when we went over the top?"

"What was the general doing, Dad?"

"He was as far behind the lines as he could get himself!"

I couldn't put that. Nor the story of the German night patrol whom he seized going into the wood. "Poor little bugger," Dad said, "he showed me his wallet and the photos of his family back at home in Hamburg." And then he'd strip his arm and bare his scars; and truly frightful was the wound across the middle of his arm.

I told instead how he taught me to ride: walk, trot, canter, gallop. How to hold my hands and grip with my knees. "Quietly does it," he said.

Quietly I sometimes went to peer with pride at his name on the war memorial that stood outside the Red House Farm. Pte Thomas Davies MM, it said.

I was just debating whether to tell how his medals were stolen from under his drunken nose one night when my thoughts were cut short. There was a knock at the front door.

"See who that is!" my mother called. I opened the door to the unlit hall.

"It's Sergeant Lamb."

"I know," I said. I knew the voice. How friendly some policemen were! "It's Sergeant Lamb from Knockin, Mum." The sooty oil lamp frowned in the sitting-room, newly lit. The darkness frowned outside.

"Disorderly and drunk again . . ." I heard between the groanings of the wind and the closing of the door. "If he'd keep off the beer . . ." My mother never said a word. ". . . I'm sure he'd be . . ." A jet of flame shot up the lamp. "We'll keep him in a bit."

I wrote on the bottom of my essay: "He's just been arrested", and went with John to milk. Emrys would come and help; Emrys who sang "The Bells of Aberdovey". He was always ready to help, as he was ready to sing.

The weeks went by, the nights drew in. Six mornings a week we went to school, then to the pictures or the baths in the afternoon — except on Saturday when I had to rush home, catch Topsy the pony and, throwing myself into the saddle, gallop like the Wild Horseman to Nesscliffe for my weekly encounter with Miss Dexter, my piano teacher, who made me play scales in contrary motion without dislodging the penny she placed on each of my wrists. I could keep it on my wrist but she never put the penny in my hand.

One Saturday in October, Mother, John, Laura and Belle had gone to town to see the film *The Drum*. I came home from my music lesson to find a little boy with steel-rimmed spectacles sitting by our kitchen fire, watching my father making toast.

"What do you do this foor?" he asked, ignoring me.

"Lord A'mighty," my father exclaimed, coughing and scattering ash on the toast. "I'm doin' it for you, for yer tea!" Dad was an expert at making toast (though it did sometimes taste of cigarettes). There were times when I wondered why he ever went out, as Mother said, "drinking and carrying on". He was such a good companion by the fire at night.

"This is our little evacuee," he said, turning to me. "Billy . . . What's yer name?"

"Foulkes," said Billy, but it sounded like Fooks to us.

"Fooks — we call that Fowks, round 'ere," said my father. Billy gave a shrug and buried his head in a *Beano*. "He came this afternoon," Dad said to me. "From Liverpool."

"Wallasey," said Billy, not raising his head.

Dad put beef dripping on his own toast and more than the ration of butter on ours. We swallowed it, hot and sticky, swilling it down with strong, sweet tea. Then we went out to milk.

"What d'you do this foor?" Billy had never seen cows being milked before and really thought milk came out of bottles and cans. I showed him my mousetrap by the

116

corn bin. He had never seen a dead mouse staring popeyed into the afterlife.

"'Oly'ead, Lundun, Shoosb'ry, Bascherch — we'e'e's Livapule?" he asked when I showed him the brilliant yellow AA sign that shone like a sun on the cover of my village book.

"I dunno," I said, "near 'Oly'ead, I sh'think."

"Woy isn't it on the soyn?" I couldn't answer that. So I passed it off by saying, "The sign's gone anyway. All our signs have gone. They might be useful to the enemy!"

"Can you make S?" He squinted up at me through little blue, forget-me-not eyes.

"Yes," I said — assuming he meant what I thought.

"D'you know what we call the Maresey gol'fish, eh?" Again I guessed and thought of higher things.

"Wot d'ya do with yer mooney? I mean, wot d'ya do with yer time?"

"Oh, things," I said.

We joined Dad round the fireside making spills.

"What do you do this foor . . .?"

"To light the fire," said Dad, who was an artist in the making of spills. He had beautiful hands, my father, with fine filbert nails. He could take a piece of newspaper and, rolling it from one corner, finish at exactly the right place to twist the end and make a firm, straight spill. Mine always came out loose and bent and had to be done again.

I knew what Dad was doing it for. He had told me. The hedge clippings ("brushings" we called them) had

117

to be burnt. We usually piled them by the pit for the bonfire on 5 November. This year, he said, we'd have to burn them in the afternoon. "The fifth'll be a Sunday," he said, counting on his fingers and curling each clean shapely nail into the palm of his hand. "No sense in 'avin' fireworks." But his eyes and cigarette still brightened at the prospect of a good blaze. He'd need a magazine of spills.

At seven o'clock I had to go to choir practice at the parsonage. "Mercy and truth are met together," we sang, "righteousness and peace have kissed each other . . ." I loved singing: psalms, responses, even the Lord's Prayer all on one note. But best I loved the high, high hymns. We had "Jerusalem the golden, with milk and honey blest". I waited for "I know not, O, I know not . . ." to come and then let fly! "What joys await us there!" My favourite hymn was "Christian up and smite them", but we only had that once in Lent. Miss Heavens, who led the choir, put her hand to her ear in dismay and visibly struggled to stay in tune.

Jimmy Roberts and I met up later that evening and let her bicycle tyres down. "An' that'll make 'er go flat!" said he.

"Surry ah, it'll an' all!" said I.

I came home to find John and the others back from town, taking Billy Foulkes in hand. Four-eyes had found the cupboard under the stairs where Mother kept her Bathbrick and Mutt, the house cat, lay confined with her kittens among the dusters, Mansion polish and black lead. Poor, harassed Mutt! Billy

118

couldn't leave her kittens alone. They swam over his arms in blind confusion till she took them, one by one, scruff o' the neck, to the barn next door.

"Don't moither 'm!" said John. "Stop briveting!"

"Wot's brivetin'?"

"Pokin' yer nose in." Here Fowksy, as we'd immediately begun to call him, hitched up his little wet nose and poked behind his glasses for a tear. "The mother'll forsake 'm an' then they'll be cowd an' 'ungry — clemmed to dyeth."

"Wot's clemmed?"

"Clemmed means starved." Billy shrank a foot. "Frittened means frightened. Ketch means catch. And larn means learn and teach. That'll larn ya! Do, mon, ya noggin-yedded nyowkin!"

Billy smiled and, pointing again to the frailty of his specs, showed that he was learning fast. "Ya moona 'it meh!" he said.

"Ya munna say dunna, it inna polite," said Laura.

"An' ya canna say wunna, cos that inna right," chimed Belle.

Billy taught us Newmarket and, after baths by the fire, we curled up on the screen with old *Beanos* and *Dandys* which he had brought from Liverpool.

That night the attic was turned into a bedroom and Mother decided that Billy should sleep in the same room as John.

"You sleep in the attic," she said to me. "Billy will not want to sleep by himself."

Had Mother forgotten my fear of the dark?

Billy went boldly ahead, not even waiting for John. "Put your hand around the candle flame — the draughts will blow it out!" John hissed.

Past the dreaded cellar door and up the first stairway we went, our shadows leaping on the walls. All good fun in company.

"Good night," I said at the tunnel door and continued on my own up two more flights of creaking old oak stairs. The shadows plunged and leapt more menacingly now. I put my hand round the candle flame to guard it from the ever stronger, colder draughts. The flame guarded me; and I guarded the flame.

As children we had the most tender relationship with candles. Alive in the darkness, you suddenly realized how friendly were those yellow flames. Unfortunately their lives and ministries were short. The darkness comprehended us. We had flashlights in reserve . . .

I mounted the top stairs as if for the last time, all imaginable fears at my heels, and only felt safe when I blew the candle out, pulled the bedclothes over my head, switched on my flashlight and took *Black Beauty* by the reins.

November. Swirling mist and fog. It seemed that not even double summertime nor all the Articles of Religion could save us from the encircling gloom. Mr Parrott, strangely sombre at Harvest Festival, was more so at Remembrance. "The one shall be taken, and the other left," he said. Martinmas came with its "Martin lowly, saint most holy, pray for us thy children"; and every Sunday now we miserable sinners knelt through the Litany and prayed: "From battle, murder and sudden death, good Lord deliver us." We were clamped in gunmetal gloom.

The cows lay in their beds of straw and dung. The pit froze. The pig was killed. An air of desolation hung about the farm. Only a hundred years before we would have salted down beef and mutton as well.

Some mornings we were so cold cycling to school that Laura cried. It was no use turning back. We tried that once. Mother waved the broom and said, "Get off with you — and if you miss the bus you'll have to cycle all the way!" We did.

"Why are you late?"

"I had to bike, sir."

"Why did you have to cycle?"

"I missed the buz."

"Why did you miss the bus?"

"I had to milk."

Whisky Johnny said no more.

One of the advantages of sleeping alone in the attic was that I raced through the whole of *A Tale of Two Cities* in one week. I was able to tell my friends Tim Kite, Maurice More and Alwyn Dyson how I saw Sydney Carton go to the guillotine while searchlights from the nearby Nibs Heath battery raked the skies and crossed my attic window, bombers droning overhead.

Tim was a beautiful pagan who slung out his hips and leant over the hall balcony like a West Midlands Show judge, easing himself off his shooting stick to take a long, level look at a line of Shropshire sheep. He was much given to thought, with an inner life which was as yet a closed, a secret book.

Maurice More only seemed to be doing nothing. It was he who spurred me on to read *A Tale*. Both he and Alwyn Dyson belonged to church choirs in the town. Our music master, Woodbine Willie, found this out and asked them to sing alternate verses of "The Holly and the Ivy". Coming as I did from an unfrocked village choir in which I was the one incomparable boy, the sound of those true treble voices hit me as a revelation. Tim pushed out his hips a bit further, and I withdrew my horns. He was a magnificent devil, but the other two were gods . . . In almost every way they were ahead of me: in street wisdom, social relationships, aircraft recognition and the knowledge of books.

My favourite book was still *Black Beauty*. I read it and re-read it. It was old familiar ground to me: the orchard at Birtwick, the pleasant meadow with its pond of clear water, the plantation of trees . . . John Manly, Jerry Barker, Joe Green were as real to me as Robin Turner, Alf Jones and Bill Rodgers who worked on farms in Little Ness. Dad only read the *Farmers Weekly*. Billy Foulkes read *Dan Dare* and *Beanos*; my brother ranged through *Rovers, Wizards, Hotspurs, Tarzan, Conrad, Two Years before the Mast, The Coral Island* and *Westward Ho!* I had not yet heard the call of the sea.

As for poetry, I had learnt "Young Lochinvar" and "Play up, play up and play the game" — without knowing who wrote it or what it was called. It was dinned into me by Miss Hyles. So, when Whisky Johnny dished out *A Book of Narrative Verse* saying, in his usual way, "Read as much as you can of *The Rime of the Ancient Mariner*," I did not know what to expect. Tim looked at me with gloom in his normally grey eye and lifted his haunch right over the edge of his seat.

"Try to be the first that ever burst into that silent sea," the chirpy Johnny sang.

I did not know what to make of: "An ancient Mariner meeteth three Gallants bidden to a wedding feast, and detaineth one . . ." But as soon as I got the picture of the Mariner with his long grey beard and glittering eye, I gave up the gloss and drank it down neat. Image after image bounced off the retina, almost too fast for the brain to sort them out; but in all that mesmeric detail there was much that was strangely familiar. The shift of tense and tension, the contrary forces exerted by the main story against the urgent business of the Wedding Guest, the strange idea of going south and getting colder — all the subtle mental surprises — were eased by the occasional lull of green pastures and still waters: the little birds' sweet jargoning, the pleasant noise of the hidden brook in the leafy month of June. The interjections of the Wedding Guest kept me on my toes as much as the buttonholing Mariner's all-out attack. The changing pace, the music fascinated me. After the terror, the marriage feast and the walk together to the kirk with a goodly company. That seemed like Little Ness.

I identified the slimy things that crawled in the rotting deep as the slow-worms that coiled themselves

123

together in the dungheaps on the farm. More than anything I recognized the

> one that on a lonesome road doth walk in fear and
>   dread,
> And having once turned round walks on
> and turns no more his head;
> Because he knows, a frightful fiend
> Doth close behind him tread.

I knew the sudden crack, the growl of ice on the pond when I broke it with an axe to allow the cattle to drink. "And ice, mast-high, came floating by as green as emerald" — that was like a film! I didn't know what an Albatross was, but ignorance enhanced the terror. And so much greater was my pity when it was killed.

The spirit that followed under the waters, the lonesome spirit requiring vengeance, who grieved for the dead Albatross, made me think of the Benedicite: "O ye Whales, and all that move in the waters, bless ye the Lord." The whole of the Benedicite is in that poem: "O ye Sun and Moon (and one bright star within the nether tip), O ye Winds, ye Fire and Heat, ye Frost and Cold, ye Ice and Snow, ye Lightnings and Clouds . . ."

And then the homecoming: the seraph band, the Hermit of the Wood, the church on the hill, the little vesper bell and — most stunningly shot of all Coleridge's filmic scenes — when the wedding guests, the bride and all appear in the garden and "the bride-maids singing are".

★   ★   ★

Everybody agreed that the *Ancient Mariner* was good. Maurice had several ideas: it was a kaleidoscope; it was like a Viking saga, as if Eric the Red had outdone Captain Cook; it was a parable worked out in old stained glass.

I said it was like a film. Alwyn said he couldn't believe that slime and leprosy and flickering grave-lights could be turned into poetry with such power. Tim liked the part when four times fifty men dropped one by one and every soul, "it passed me by, like the whizz of my cross-bow." He relished

> The owlet whoops to the wolf below,
> That eats the she-wolf's young.

And the whistling hag with the red lips, the Night-Mare Life in Death who thicks man's blood with cold. "She who diced for the souls of the crew," added Johny. He said that of all the poems in the book, this was the one we would always remember.

What Whisky Johnny didn't say and I didn't realize of course, is that it is a very religious poem. And I was at heart, if not in mind and body, a very religious child.

125

CHAPTER
FIVE

"Eileen, teach these boys to dance!"

After school one Saturday morning late in November I bolted my lunch, flew to Nesscliffe for my music lesson, visited my aunt Nellie Thonger, and still had time to collect wood for the fire.

It is nearly true that I flew. I galloped the grey pony down the Rock Lane, my music rolled up and tied to the saddle with string. It burst at speed and scattered itself in all directions. I was, as usual, late.

After I had put the pony in the stable, Miss Dexter said, "Have you shut the gate? You are rather late." She then left me to practise my scales.

When at last she came in she gave me a sight-reading test, full of accidentals including double sharps. "Now 'Album for the Young'," she said. She heard me play "A Sad Story" (twice) and "The Poor Orphan" (three times). "Can't you put a little more expression into it?" she asked. "It's rather sad, you see."

Finally I attempted to plunge through the double octaves of Rachmaninoff's C-sharp Minor Prelude and at this point Miss Dexter withdrew her white, attenuated hands and let me go early to my aunt, who knew just what boys like: caraway seedcake, straight from the oven.

Her home, Oak Cottage, had an inglenook, a tiled and polished floor. Hams hung in muslin bags from hooks overhead and a warming pan, a copper kettle, a barometer and a long clock glowed in the evening light. Of all our courtesy aunts, Nellie Thonger was perhaps the most wonderful. She had an inner and outer stillness achieved by long experience as the licensee of Nesscliffe Hotel. She was round and warm, seeming to be wrapped entirely in soft wool, her silver hair tidied over her head in a bun, the shape of a perfect cottage loaf. And she always had the teapot to hand.

Huge Uncle John was her brother, bearded, rubicund and permanently wreathed in smiles. His boots resounded on the tiles with a heavy, hobnailed tread. He had a chair to match his ample form and as soon as he was settled, his stick within reach, he would stretch out a hand the size of a plate of meat for a basin of tea; but he always drank it from the saucer with a slow, deliberate slurp, putting the cup where he could see it, cooling at his side.

He blew bubbles round his beard, cooling what was in his saucer, his blue eyes mischievously bleared like fishes' in a tank. He boomed and bubbled as he drank, laying down the law about the market price of milk, of corn, of his beautiful, pampered strawberry-roan cows . . .

I just had time to look at *The Deerslayer* before my aunt said, "Another cup of tea? Another piece of cake?"

Shuffling to the oven door she was delighted to find another cake had risen. All done by touch. Poor Nellie, she had gone blind.

So, full of seedcake, I came home, unsaddled the pony and, dropping my music where I wouldn't be able to find it, went sticking with Florrie.

Florrie was the cowman's daughter and, quite simply, she had india-rubber bones. She was as tough as nails and twice as nimble. She could dance the hornpipe.

We set off on our rambles with a Uveco sack. These sacks, which were used for bran or flaked maize, were huge and therefore ideal for stuffing with wood.

Florrie, with her towy hair, dark-shadowed eyes and somewhat sawn-off, milk-white teeth, was my ideal hauling companion. We would cheerfully range over the fields as far as Neighbour Martin's copse, where the pheasants stalked in quietness and the gathering was good.

But before we reached the coppy, we picked up carob fruits (or locusts) placed in sheep troughs on the way, as sweet and toothsome on a cold November day as nougat or the toffee Florrie's mother made. A thundery glow hung in the sky: the glow that comes before a fall of snow. And Florrie's eyes looked violet-blue. "Would you go deep inside there, by yourself?" she asked me, pointing to the darkly silhouetted wood. I funked the test.

"Oh ho, your eyes are green!" she laughed, full in my face. She smelled of locusts, flake maize and sweet tea. I didn't challenge her. I knew she'd go.

★　★　★

"Let's go to the whist drive at Nesscliffe," Mother said, one evening out of the blue. She probably thought she would not have much more free time with Christmas looming up.

"Yes, let's," said Billy, who had never played whist but was eager to learn. John said "Let's not", and I wasn't sure. The girls were curled up in two easy chairs by the fire intent on reading *Anne of Green Gables* and *What Katy Did Next*.

I took a gamble. While Mother rooted out her old fur coat, Billy and I struggled into boots and scarves and Balaclavas: I from muffled gallantry, he from simple curiosity. With cries of "Where's the flash!" we forsook the kindly lights of home. Never was scene so changed.

Hist! Whist! A whistle thin — and pencilled in the moonless mist three figures: Mother, Billy and me.

"Come on, you two, or we'll be late!" Mother shone her torch on Billy in a cloud of steam. "Really!" Silence, and another uphill trudge. "And if he says 'No trumps', play your ace . . ." She shone her light on Billy, dimpled and ready to emit another whistle betokening assent. He could express more that way than he could in words. "But follow suit — and don't lead with the Icing! And try to remember what's gone before. And . . ."

Ahead, the lights of the AS, dimmed for the blackout, told us we were near the village hall. We were swallowed up in a pall of comforting smoke as we crouched, eyes down, over our cards, dextrously dealt on tables topped with baize.

129

"Hearts are trumps." Our voices melted into a sea of silent awe. I had only one: the king. My lady partner, stony-faced, led with the ace. I followed suit. The silence deepened into gloom.

"Did you know they were trumps?" I asked. No answer. The oil lamp readjusted its flame. But we moved on. She had all the hearts, her own and mine.

And here and there a partner's less than stony look helped me advance by modest sevens and eights, but never nine as in that first bright game. I had become as taciturn and poker-faced during play as the rest, stealing between tables, teetering above the waterline in the struggle to progress.

But who was this? A whistle thin, and Billy, white-faced, dimpled in, his cowlick stiff with brilliantine, his sharp eyes glinting behind glasses secured with wire and wool, his whistle giving nothing much away.

"No trumps!" He led with an ace and picked up tricks as if with a magnet. And he went on while I, fingering my frown, stayed there. And then the last hand — the cards were signed; checking done, the chat resumed. The MC announced the winning lady. "And the winning gentleman: Billy Foulkes." A low whistle, a Wallasey "Wow!" and Billy went up to claim the goose.

"Oh, not another goose to pluck," my mother sighed.

Drama was sudden and nearly always sanguinary on our farm: castration, pig killing, calving, farrowing — and the plucking of the Christmas geese. Mother told me that as a young farmer's bride she had held the geese behind her while my father cut their throats. And now, as every year, when winter drew over us and darkness tried to shut us in, I came home one day to a miasma of singed feathers and a sense of desolation. (You don't have to see death on a farm, you can feel it: something is missing.) And under a cloud of feathers I found my mother snapping and stripping — the sound was like an elastoplast being torn away — first the wings and then the bodies of those fifteen-pound-weight ghosts of geese.

She had her old brown beret on, fluted like a jelly mould but dusted over with fluff. And an old mac that never saw the light of day, with a sack drawn over her knees. And on the sack were the orange feet of the goose spread out to one side; on the other the head hung down with an accusing eye. The feathers floated aloft, securing themselves in every grey cobweb of the old barn, or, lighting, ran along the ground.

"Just tidy up those breasts for me — I have another two to do," my mother said.

I rolled a piece of paper up and, setting it alight, I singed the pink and yellow stippled skin. The lantern, set swinging on a beam, exaggerated the cavernous bowels of the old building and through the tickling, feathered air we talked in clouds of steam.

"I've several wreaths to make tonight ..." Her furred-up eyes suggested that I should go and find some holly, moss and bits of baling wire. "And you'll just catch the post if you go now. I've done the Christmas things. And shut the fowl up on your way or there are some will never roost again! And ..."

I left her quilted, muffled like a ghost, too deep, too deft, too diligent, too practised to put off what could still be done that night.

A few days later my mother said, "When you go to the wood see if you can find a Christmas tree. Not too big — just the top off one would do."

I mentioned it to Florrie, who smiled beguilingly; and, with a saw beneath my coat, two preternaturally old figures floated silently round the penumbra of the copse. We could just make out the shapes of pheasants and hear their wings soft-shuffle overhead. Indian-file, we penetrated the dark heart of the wood, Florrie leading soundlessly, I two steps behind. "Here's one," she lisped. "Gi'me the saw!" And before I could focus she was halfway up the tree and sawing fast. Beneath a baleful moon, we dragged our timber back, fearful of whom we might meet.

My mother was delighted with the tree. "Take it to the school tomorrow," she said. "But tell Miss Hyles the donor wishes to remain anonymous."

The following Friday night, the little schoolroom lit with unaccustomed cheer, the audience gathered, Neighbour Martin and the other landowners prominent in the front seats, the Christmas tree aglow, the hornpipe began. Our mothers were smiling wonderingly at Florrie's effervescent glee and india-rubber bones as up the mast she went again, then down, and heel-and-toe she climbed imaginary air, descended, backed, unrolled her arms, then hauling on the

132

bowline, climbed aloft. She ravelled everybody in her india-rubber charms.

Miss Hyles, hand on heart at the piano after keeping pace with all these accelerations, thanked the unknown donor of the Christmas tree.

There was more to come, but of all the items, expected and unexpected, only one could match, we thought, our Florrie and her hornpipe.

"One, two, three, four, *five* and six, sing the bells of Aberdovey." Emrys, his hands threaded across his waistcoat, was counting and recounting his memories of the bells. Is there anything, we wondered, more surprising to the ear than a big voice in a little room?

He sang,

"I'll cross the sea once more, and love come
    knocking at my door,
And little loves and hopes shall fly around us in
    a covey
When we're married, you and I, at home in
    Aberdovey."

There we were cooped up in the cramped little schoolroom; everyone who was not at the back was much too near the fire. We sat through an evacuee lady's haw-haw rendering of "How Now, Brown Cow" (guffaws from the lads at the back); a farmer's daughter playing the violin ("the tune the old cow died of," my naughty mother said); the parson commending our "variety" (he thanked us for our money); the Second

Minuet (what would the third be like?); "The tender blossom on the tree" — and now, at last!

Emrys was recalled. A cough, apologetic but controlled; the beaming, bow-tied, bachelor bass stepped forth. He had, he said, no more "ditties". He would sing "The Bells" again. I was transported. An exile, in America perhaps, I shared his *hiracth* (longing) with him; *cariad* (darling) was the only Welsh word in the translation that he sang, but it was enough. However few drops of Welsh blood I had in my veins, my heart leapt up. This simple diatonic counting cast its spell, compelling all. It silenced the shuffling figures on the ridged and furrowed benches. The fuggy haze dissolved. The room, the raftered roof, the fireguard, the smell of corduroy — all disappeared. The air assumed romance. I only saw through tear-blurred eyes my old friend Emrys, smiling and sincere, counting and recounting "The Bells of Aberdovey".

Two nights before Christmas, Mother said, "You and John can take this cake to Lizzie at The Shruggs." Lizzie was our old washerwoman. She lived in an umbra of larch trees and bracken on the way to Nesscliffe Hill. Dark was the only word for The Shruggs. You could hardly see inside the two-roomed house; but there was a fire with pots bubbling and brewing round the hearth, and cats and sepia photographs and a settle and rag rugs.

Outside there was a tin shed, frosted over, where Lizzie's husband kept two cows. "Distant in time as Palestine," said John. We were given a Christmas tree to take back. "From under the hill," said Lizzie, knowing that Mother liked her tree to come from there. And on the way back we worked out a poem:

> Distant in time as Palestine
> Two Shorthorn cows lay down
> In a buckled shed,
> Its split-larch frame
> With corrugated iron spread
> And fir trees stood around.
>
> And hessian sacks were stuffed in gaps
> And bale wire hung on hooks,
> But contentedly
> The cows lay down
> From draught and dampness almost free
> Though frost winked on the ground.

"Those cows live as well as their owners," said John. "Surprising, though, how snug a cattle shed can be."

I put the poem in my village book when I got home. And marked The Shruggs on the map.

"Bluedy 'ell," said Billy when he realized that because Christmas Eve had fallen on Sunday it meant he would have to go to church on Monday as well.

"We used to have three services on a Sunday," I said to calm him down. "Now we have only two because of the blackout. Evensong used to be at six-thirty."

"Sex-therty?" said Billy. "Yeh must uv spent all dee in cherch!"

135

"Just think," I said, "no Litany! And numbers fifty-nine and sixty-two!"

"What's sexty-two?"

"'While shepherds watched'."

"'Their ternip tops . . .' Shall I sing yeh the Livapule varesion?"

We spent the evening dressing the Christmas tree with tinsel and clip-on candles and putting the decorations up. Sleep never came easily to me in the attic; and Father Christmas, I noticed, smoked the same Players cigarettes as last year, still coughed, but spent less time on her rounds. In the morning we found our stockings were pillow-cases and they contained not chocolate watches and tangerines or sugar mice but *White Fang* and a lambsfoot knife for John, *Tales of a Log Cabin* and a brummock (billhook) for Billy, and a set of mathematical instruments and Clementi's *Gradus Ad Parnassum* for me. For the girls there were *Little Women* and *Little Men* bulked up with materials for knitting, sewing and making wool rugs.

"Bluedy 'ell," said Billy, inspecting his brummock. "What's this?"

"A brummock."

"Well, what's it foor?"

"For chopping sticks!" Billy, always reluctant to do his share, was guided to the Yule log in the shed.

"Look sharp!" called Mother. "You'll need to get ready for church."

"Christians, awake! Salute the happy morn . . ."

The church, of course, was a picture: the lid of the font was lapped with cloth as white as snow and ringed with berried holly, blood-bright red; the little thatched crib smelt of hay and candle wax, and the figures, brought, someone said, from Jerusalem, had been adoringly placed in exactly the same positions, in order, as last year.

Miss Dowty said, "Good morning-g!" and Mrs Darby, holding on to her companion, shuffled in, dwindling and deaf, her frame weighed down with astrakhan and drenched with scent, but armed with a stick and an ear trumpet and still able to make herself heard.

"O Lord, raise up (we pray Thee) Thy power, and come among us." We were regenerate. We were renewed. Even Jimmy Roberts's ears were clean. For Christmas was the time of purification. "Because thou didst give Jesus Christ to make us clean from all sin . . ." Mr Parrott, more pink and white than ever in his crimson maniples and stole, preached on his favourite themes, the Incarnation and the Atonement; alternative sides, he called them, of the same precious coin. It was, even to an eleven-year-old, all blessedly familiar. The Darbys and the Davieses, the Birchalls and the Balderstons, the Westons and the Westaways, all took their well-remembered parts. Or if not they, their ghosts.

And Mr Parrott, who seldom strayed from the strict observance of the liturgy, put on a more human face and wished us all a happy Christmas. He seemed a rather lonely bachelor priest, aloof and dignified. It was not his style to stand at the door and shake hands with everybody after the service.

The boys came out in bright new socks and slunk to muted horseplay by the lych gate steps; tugging ties and teasing one who, at fourteen, had just gone into longs. "Who's dropped ya? Eh?" Distant mothers forgot themselves and stayed behind to praise the decorations in the church till fathers puffed their cheeks and stamped their feet and steered us home. "Got to do justice to the *bird*, Mother!"

The season's greetings were exchanged again, not once, not twice, but many times.

After the socials and the whist drives came the untried pleasures of the dance. Before the twelve days of Christmas were out and the decorations taken down, Mother saw the chance of getting us from under foot. "Eileen, teach these boys to dance," she said. Eileen was often at our house for tea. The eldest of the Chesneys, Eileen was good-looking and athletic, with a prefect's badge on her gymslip and a look of confidence in her clear blue eyes. The front room furniture was thrown back and the grandfather clock leant forward on to the arm chair in astonishment at the sight.

"Left foot, right foot, one, two, three . . . Left foot — no, the other one! Head up! Slow, slow, quick-quick, slow . . ." Eileen held me, like a rubber leek, trying to straighten me up. "No, don't look down." (I was trying to see where my feet were — they didn't seem to be in the same room.)

"You steer me!" she said. I couldn't steer myself. By the time I had corrected the left foot, the right was in the way. Or *her* left. Or *her* right. I couldn't see over her shoulder, Eileen being tall and getting bigger every day.

"No, don't lean back!" I must have been as awkward as a fence post. I stumbled through the chassés and reverses and earned a breather while Billy and my brother took the floor. He, unmusical John, was better than I. That was all the spur I needed. Besides, you learn by watching someone good.

And so on New Year's Eve we went, not to Nesscliffe or Baschurch or Ruyton-XI-Towns but to Mytton and Fitz, in the moonlight.

Our bicycles needed no lights; our front lamps no gloves to shield their beams. If there was a drone of bombers overhead we hardly heard it for the scarves wound round our ears. The searchlights swept the sky. No bombs would ever be dropped on Merrington, Mytton and Fitz. Our aerodrome would see to that. And there was the Perry, a thread of silver below the bridge, under the hill-set village, the ghostly church — all in a wash of moonlight.

The village hall, small and intimate, was balmy with beer, cigarettes, Brylcreem and scent. We thought it was the Alhambra.

There were military two-steps, veletas, quick-steps and a tango, which we, as novices, sat out. But one girl, dancing the tango with true Spanish zest, and smiling as she stepped, had caught my eye. I had, I knew, seen her before. She had a bonny, bouncing head of hair. She worked, I remembered, at the road-builder's office at Montford Bridge, near where we caught the bus for school. She smiled again.

It was one of those myths about dancing that the girl you chose for the last waltz was the one you considered the best. It was not yet twelve o'clock but the time was ticking by. A quick-step was announced. I dashed to get my girl. "Delighted," she said, and smiled.

The rest is a dream.

I never danced so well as with that girl. We chasséd and cornered and put in little fancy bits with unselfconscious ease. She was firm and I was firm. She overcame my shyness and we whirled and twirled as one. No word did we speak. And at the end she smiled and went back to her friends.

"Ambitious, ain't yer?" said Wallesey Will, a slight snigger under his steamed-up specs. He was a better dancer than any of us. "Nice bitta skeert!"

But she didn't dance the last waltz with me or Billy or any of us, but with a young flying officer for whom perhaps this would be the last year. All through "Auld Lang Syne" she was opposite me but singing and smiling and teasing him with a cup o' kindness in her eye.

Two weeks later she again came into view. I was waiting at the bus stop. She whizzed down the hill on her all-steel Raleigh bike, her bonny hair still bouncing behind. She waved through fingerless mitts a hand I would gladly have clasped.

"Come on," said John, "the bus is 'ere."

I nearly missed the bus. And wished I had.

Mother with her conjuror's gift of surprise had decided to defy the blackout and take us to see a travelling

140

repertory company performing *East Lynne*. She said it was based on the book by Mrs Henry Wood. "I won't tell you the story . . . You'll enjoy it — and I shall have a good weep!" So, one chilly January evening we all set off on the two-mile walk to Ruyton-XI-Towns; all, that is, except one, who was mysteriously already there.

Sparks flew from my brother's hobnail boots as we clattered along the Ruyton road, breaths steaming in the frosty air.

"There's the Plough," said Mother, pointing fixedly to the sky.

"There's Orion," said I, airily waving my arm about.

"Cassiopeia!" shouted John.

"Spell it!" Laura shouted back.

"Look it up when you get home." Mother brought us down to earth.

Past Hawleys' cottage and the Millingtons', up hill, down dale, Billy and I strove to keep up with John. We passed Queen's Court where the boys we called "the Darlings" lived, as old as us but "nesh", meaning soft.

"I don't think they'll be coming out," said John. "Too cold for them."

"The wind would freeze their little pink knees . . ."

"That's quite enough!" My mother cut my poem off as we went panting up another hill. The trees were black, square blocks of Norway spruce. Beyond them lay the Cliffe, a sandstone giant huddled under spent tatters of heather, rags of gorse. "That's where the gyppos are," I breathed at John.

"'The raggle-taggle gypsies O,'" he breathed back, threateningly. I wanted to keep on his right, to be

141

nearer Jack Moyle's white fold gates. His house, Birch Park, was like a castle. The moon, like a milk-white steed, rose up above the chimney tops. The road ran downhill now, well-lit and shadowless and safe. From here you could smell the Oddfellows Hall.

We reached the doors which opened to a wall of warmer air. Smoke hung like a cloak inside.

"One and four halves," my mother said, and added, "Please."

The lady sitting there in green velvet, make-up, rings and bangles, rose. "Mod'm," she said, "your seats are complimentary! None but the best!"

She showed us down the aisle. We fell into our seats. And then stood up. "God save the King," we sang, to a wailing wind-up gramophone. We settled down again. My mother's fur was warm and fuzzy by my ear, and I could smell all kinds of scents; some friendly, some more strange.

"It's the make-up and scenery," said Laura.

"Grease paint," said John.

"Mook," said Billy, who had learnt a new word and spread it universally. He might have meant the paint and powder. He might have meant the play.

The lights kept going down. The lady on the stage was always looking in the mirror. And Mr Carlyle, the wealthy hero, was very artificial, twirling his dark moustache.

Then, in a fuller light, we saw our pretty little sister Belle. She'd combed her hair and changed her voice. She only had to kneel and say a few words while the

Lady Isabel patted her head. Mother kept screwing up her handkerchief.

"How long does it go on?" I asked.

"Till eternity," said the oily Mr Carlyle.

"'Dead, and never called me Mother'," Mother sighed, repeating the last line softly to herself.

"Thank goodness that's the end," said John.

"Sissy stoof," said Billy. We knew he meant the play.

We hardly knew what the play was about, but when Belle came home with stars in her eyes we asked her how much she had been paid.

"Ssh!" our mother said. "The reward is in the doing, you know. It's an honour to be asked."

I gabbled my prayers in bed that night: "Bless all kind friends, makemeagoodboyAmen." Then, getting out of bed and down on my knees, I added, "Please God, help me to make my fortune." I knew that money wasn't everything, but I could have done with a little of Mr Carlyle's.

The happy and prosperous New Year that people had warmly talked about had crashed on ice. In February deep snow blocked the roads. I had to fetch bread once from Ruyton on my pony. Bravely Topsy breasted the drifts. But it was touch and go. As I urged her on with my knees, cold, crunchy crystals crept into my wellingtons, condensing round my feet. Parts of my body were on fire; parts paralysed. But we struggled on. The baker had an unexpected customer that day. "Don't eat the crust," he said, handing me an appetizing, warm and well-baked loaf. Topsy, wheeling, rolled a knowing eye and steamed for home.

I wished the baker had not said, "Don't eat the crust." It made temptation that much harder to resist.

As for my own prosperity, I turned my money over at sight of the new moon; but I still had the same old money left. I gave up my Woodbines and winegums; but such sacrifices did not make you rich. If they had done the war would have made us all millionaires.

The only means I had of making my fortune was Dertie Gertie, as Billy Foulkes called my little pink pig. I had bantams but we always ate the eggs. I had pigeons and puppies but they never brought anything in. My mother would not have agreed, of course; they brought in dirt. And so did my pig. From being a little pink orphan, the runt of the litter, wrapped in flannel in a shoe box by the fire, Dertie Gertie became demanding and impossible. She walked where Mutt and angels feared to tread. But she could not be put in a sty with other pigs. "They'd take the curl out of 'er tail," my father had threatened darkly. "Ya canna put a cade lamb back with the flock — it's the same with a pig. Put 'er in the loose box by 'erself."

It was this that made me decide to sell Gertie. I couldn't bear the squeals of my little pet porker cooped up in a place by herself. And I couldn't put her at risk with the other pigs to be hounded from the trough and have her ears and tail bitten off. One way and another she would starve or fret to death.

The answer to my prayer came the following Saturday, in the shape of Charlie Onions in his blue and white apron bearing a basket of beef. "I'll give you thirty shillings for her now," he said. And Gertie ended the day in Baschurch on a butcher's bench smelling of scrubbed wood and sawdust and trimmed with parsley, cleaner in death than she had ever been, except in her pink dawn life.

I had never had thirty shillings before — and didn't know what to do with it. I couldn't put it with my threepenny bits. I put it in my bed.

"Peter always makes his own bed in the morning," Mother mischievously announced at lunch the next day. Was she wise to me?

"Creep," said my brother.

"Sissy boy," said Bill.

"So you can follow suit! And I'm tired of lugging slop pails up and down those stairs, so you can take it in turn to do that too. Eldest first." John looked at me with hurt and vengeful eyes. Billy took his steamed-up glasses off. The girls just laughed. "There's nothing to laugh at," said Mother. "Get on with your dinner. And when you've finished you can clean out the henhouses. I want to whitewash them this afternoon."

Spring cleaning came early to farms. Lured by bright sun but stung by keen winds, with rosy cheeks and tingling ears, we cast away the works of darkness and put upon us the armour of light. Our annual scrape, my brother called it. With a wheelbarrow loaded with spades we clattered over the cobbles, across the road and down the fields to the henhouses where Rhode Island reds, Leghorns and rose-combed Wyandottes sat

145

cramped on perches dropping their droppings and keeping up a low-toned conversation with closed eyes. As the days lengthened they sprouted lustrous feathers, scarlet combs and stretched a trim young yellow leg. They sprang out from the bob-hole and cackled with new life.

"They're coming into lay," my mother said behind her cigarette. "Get all those perches out and clean them off. And get a bit of old hay from the bing."

"What for?" said Bill.

"To line the nesting boxes with," said John.

Even with the door open, cleaning out a henhouse is a suffocating job. We held our breath and plunged in with a shovel, scooping out the tacky-acky. *Ach y wy!* Red mites tickled noses, eyes and ears and prompted John to shout, "Unclean! Unclean!" bumping his head on the door frame as he struggled out for air.

"Scrape the perches with a knife!" said Mother, going in with a bucket of whitewash, her splashed and spattered smock, a duster round her head and tears of whitewash on her boots.

"Look what we found in the bing!" my sisters sang. "All these threepenny and sixpenny bits!"

"They're mine!" I yelled.

"They were left there by the tramp," they said. Billy was already halfway up the field to see if there were any more.

"Finders keepers," Belle chimed pompously.

"It's treasure trove," said Mother with a flick of her whitewash brush. "Owner unknown. I'll divide it equally between you and put it in the penny bank. Now where's that hay? We'll put a little in each box. And then a pot-egg in the hay."

"A nest-egg," John supposed . . .

I limped away. Defeated, it seemed, in my effort to become a millionaire.

"Never mind," I said to Mother, as we reached the door of the house. "I'll have five shillings from Aunt Alice soon!"

"Yes, for your birthday." Aunt Alice always sent us postal orders on our birthdays for that grand amount; she was a lady of independent means.

"And a Saturday penny, when she comes to stay!" I brightened up. And thought smugly of the thirty shillings tucked safely in my bed.

"Well, you might — but then again, you might not," said Mother. "Aunt Alice has written to say she may have to stay with her friend who's rather ill."

Poor friend, thought I. Aunt Alice regularly came and went. Her home was in Hoylake, the Wirral, "the right side of Liverpool", but she was presently sojourning in the Vale of Evesham — talking to the asparagus, Mother said.

Tickled all over with mites, I stripped and purged myself under the pump.

CHAPTER
SIX

"You mustn't fight . . . Just walk away, don't fight"

9 March. My birthday. Swirling winds and driving rain which tippled from our caps and spouted from the girls' brimmed hats. Surface water spurted up like fountains from our cycle wheels. Only when we reached Montford Bridge, threw down our bikes and climbed on the bus, did we realize that the Severn was in flood. It lay like Lake Ontario on the fields. We sat, our mackintoshes shrinking on our saturated frames, trying to make out landmarks through the steamed-up windows on the way: the top of Grange Bank, Bicton school, the tollhouse, Shelton watertower . . . When the driver finally stopped we were surprised to find ourselves in Frankwell, the wrong side of the Welsh Bridge. "You can walk the rest, milads," he said. And that we did. Gangplanks had been set up both sides of the bridge where the river had burst its banks. We strolled into assembly late, and much remarked upon. I wondered how Tim knew it was my birthday. "We'll

give ya the bumps," he hissed behind his hand while
"For His mercies aye endure, ever faithful ever sure"
rolled round again, verse after verse of the hymn.

"Bumps in the Dungeon," he whispered while
Whisky Johnny set out Pythagoras on the blackboard
during maths. "Twelve, is it?"

"Half past ten," said Dukes, who wasn't paying
attention.

That playtime was a misery to me. Already chapped
and sore after being soaked to the skin, I had to suffer
the bumps, dragged down uneven steps (one — bump,
two — bump) till I lay like the Count of Monte Cristo,
spread-eagled in the Chateau d'If.

The rain had stopped, but a more sinister storm was
brewing up. When I finally scrambled out I encountered
the Snooks. They were identical twins and they haunted
me in the playground at the Priory like a recurrent
dream.

Bullying at Little Ness was totally direct and
physical, and the attacker could easily be outwitted. At
the Priory it was subtle, sinuous and inescapable.

"Hello, John's brother. It's your birthday then today?
Say it's your birthday."

"It is my birthday," I replied. My interlocutor had a
long neck, half-closed eyes, a squeaky voice, ears
clipped to the sides of his head and smiled with only a
curled-up lip.

Two minutes later the same squeaky voice asked the
same question, made the same demand. Then two
identical interlocutors with identical adam's apples
rolling in identical long necks, identical half-closed

149

eyes, ears clipped to the side and curled-up lips, in unison asked.

"I said it was!" I raged. "So bugger off!" I snatched the cap off one of the Snooks and threw it into the crowd. At which they looked like the parson at Sunday school and gathered a cloud of witnesses. A gangling older lad called Gadget Sykes came up with the cap and said, "You shouldn't talk to Snook like that." I hit him on the nose and then the whole school ringed around at shouts of "Fight! A fight!" They kept the prefects off by massing round and urged us on with "'It 'im, Davies! 'It 'im, Sykes!" I didn't think I could handle Sykes, but down he went and I gave him one on the ground with my fist. "Oh, you shouldn't've 'it 'im when 'e was down . . ."

The bell had gone, just as Sykes went down. The prefect on duty hauled me off to his lair in Priory House.

I wondered if I should be sent to the Head; if I should have to stand, as my brother said the malefactors did, on that thick brown carpet, surrounded by thick, dark oak panelling, thick books and pipe-tobacco smoke, to hear the Head, a master of the monosyllable, cough and say, "Bend down, right down", and feel the cane swipe my backside. But no, I was given a double sheet of foolscap with my task already spelled out for me at the top! "I must not fight on after the bell — Queensberry Rules."

When I returned to the art room the whole class breathed in as one. Johnny was reading aloud a poem called *The Everlasting Mercy*. He did not stop, but

150

signalled his assent for me to take my seat. My attention was eagerly engaged by Masefield's fictional fight.

"How many d'ya get?" Kite asked behind his hand, thinking I had been to the Head.

"A hundred, of course," I said.

"Cor . . ."

"You mustn't fight," said John on our way home. I was riding my bike, standing on the pedals, straining the chain. I couldn't sit on the seat.

"Just walk away, don't fight," he said again when we got home. For that I decided not to show him my bumps. I would keep them to myself, nursing them jealously, guardedly, though they were in a part of my anatomy which I could not see myself.

March was cold, bright, fitful, spiteful and rough. Winds of scorn blew from the north and east. The geese yelled angrily at the shortage of grass. The cattle stood with their backs to the gale and trampled their hay into the ground. And when the winds relented, still the air was bleak and bruised, black-blue. The milk yield dropped. We stood about in extra coats; or went indoors and hugged the fire. We'd never bin so cowd.

And the week before Easter Mr Oakley came to cut our hair. To tidy us up. Dad, John, Billy and me.

Mr Oakley, a churchwarden, the old coachman at Little Ness House, was a grey Edwardian ember still burning in a polished grate; an old retainer, hallmarked, an Ancient of Days. Everything about him was solid and silver: his head, his watch and chain, his pipe with silver band and grille. Even his suit was silver and, when he "popped his jacket off", his waistcoat had a silver sheen, especially at the back. His wife, who kept him so presentable, was hardly ever seen out. She called him Father; and they lived at Quality Square.

Mr Oakley never hurried. He cut my father's hair. He cut my brother's hair. He cut the forelock off the cowlicked Foulkes who sulked; was told to grow up; didn't; and was sent to bed — in the attic. (Going to bed in the attic and growing up were synonymous.)

At last it was my turn. Mr Oakley, puffing a little, propelled me nearer the light. Nearer the window, that is, but further from the fire and its comforting glow, the centre of affairs.

"Keep still, ya young beggar, or I'll cut yer ear off!" Head pressed against a waistcoat smelling of smoke, celery and the potting shed, I did my best to endure the old coachman's monthly excursions round my head, his depredations on my hair. Mr Oakley's own hair was short, stiff, strong and straight. No model for me.

"Don't turn yer 'ead, or . . ." Mr Oakley's underlip protruded more on one side than the other, blue and bulbous with the strain of supporting a pipe for three parts of a century. He was supposed to have let the chauffeur pull one of his teeth with pliers, he sitting crosslegged on the garden seat one summer Sunday afternoon. So he was hardly likely to understand the impatient shufflings of a peevish juvenile. But my eyes were drawn to that lip, so weathered by his pipe. It had a burl, a blob, a bulge on which I focused as he spoke.

152

He finished me off. "You've got a double crown, milad. Yer 'air'll part both ways." I wondered what he meant by that.

He'd cut off all my curls. They lay around like fallen flowers. "There," he said, as he flapped the towel. "Yo'm less like a girl. Yo'll grow straight now!"

There was something about having your hair cut. It lopped your manhood off. It took your strength away. It made you shrink.

It was one of the causes of my regular regression from suavity and otherworldliness to pimply bestiality. Back in the tunnel of light, that evening, I took it out on John. Instead of merely sticking pins in him, I tried to harpoon him in bed.

"The Pouncefoots have gone to Quality Square," I said as I laid my short head on the pillow and waited for the reply. There was not even a "So what?" I would have to select another dart.

"The Pouncefoots have moved to Quality Square. They couldn't stay at Martin's farm. Their dog got in the chicken run."

"And then the feathers flew!" My crazy brother threw his pillow, leaking feathers over me.

"You are awake!" I said, surprised and spluttering injuredly. "You're very touchy about the Pouncefoots, aren't you?"

He didn't say he wasn't.

There were two of these Pouncefoot girls. They lived with their mother in the village and they went to a private school, evacuated to Ness Strange. I first saw them on a field by the Great Ness road, whacking a ball with a cross between a long-handled bat and a butterfly net. They were extremely fast, full-blooded, and — to one not interested in rules — extremely fair. "Sorray Sue" or "Sorray Ange" they shouted as they felled their opponents with their clattering crooks and hurled the ball towards the goal. The goalkeeper was petrol-blue. The rest glowed like young furnaces. When my brother told me it was lacrosse, an American Indian game, one of the fastest on earth, when he named some of the key positions like First Home, I knew he had inside information . . . And yes, he had.

Audrey, the eldest, was John's First Home. She was a budding English rose. She was a fresh-air girl. Even in winter, but more now spring was on the way, she used to ride about the village on a bicycle, slowing down when she saw me to ask where John had gone. And then, as the plot came together, he used to leave messages with me which said where he would be. It was all very Red Indian.

"It's quiet down the Cow Lane now," I said, trying to lead him on. No answer. "You won't go out for a day or two, not now your hair's so short."

He grunted like a pig. I covered up my ears and went to sleep.

Aunt Alice decided to visit us on Good Friday after all.

"How old is Aunt Alice reel-ly, Mum?" I asked.

"Don't say reel-ly. And don't Mum me. I'm your mother."

Start again. "But Mother, how old is she?"

"Ninety-five — she told you last year."

"Yes, and as old as her tongue and a little bit older than her teeth."

"Her teeth look older than her tongue," whispered John. Clout.

"Now get on with your dinner. I've got all these things to do before she comes."

Mother was not eating with the rest of us. She was cutting thin bread and butter, putting it in neat triangles on a special plate and setting a tray with a china cup and saucer, a cream jug and a sugar basin with tongs and proper sugar lumps. She called them loaves.

Mother would just about manage to clear away the dinner things and wash the floor before Charlie Parry brought Miss Cowell by taxi from Baschurch station at half past three. Then Mother would boil a fresh brown egg for three and a half minutes and take it with a piece of cold chicken with the thin bread and butter into the front room. We would not see Aunt Alice till evening.

"The nights are drawing out," my dad would say. "You'll be able to take the cows up the Ruyton road for a bit after tea." He had shaved and the shine on his face and his hair parted properly highlighted his good looks. I wished he'd always look like that. He did it for Aunt Alice. He even talked in a lower voice. But he stayed in the kitchen in his broad-backed chair with the *Farmers Weekly* and the *Wellington Journal* and *Shrewsbury News*. A big coal fire brightened molten gold in the grate. He would not go out tonight. It was like a New

155

Year resolution: tomorrow he would have forgotten about it.

The next day was Saturday, Easter Saturday. It was still cold but bright and dry. The farmyard was dry enough for Aunt Alice to step daintily in the direction of the "ship-on", as she called it. Actually she did not get to the cowhouse door until Easter Sunday morning, and then only to peep in to satisfy herself that the milk in her cream jug really did come from "those magnificent beasts", the cows clad in their coats of mail which were the accumulation of a winter's dung-impregnated straw, clinging and clanking on their sides. She had already been to Early Communion. The eggs on the breakfast table had cosies on them and beside each one, wrapped in silver paper, was a small Easter egg. Aunt Alice played the piano on the tablecloth to show off all the rings on her long yellow fingers, occasionally going off into a reckless roulade. She had so many rings on her hands you felt sorry for the odd finger that had only one.

"How is that nice Mr Brighton?" she asked, thinking of Mr Parrott.

"We passed him on the Great Ness road last week, or he passed us," my mother said. "He was on his bicycle. 'Sorry I'm not going your way,' he said. And so were we!" My mother and I had taken the bus from Shrewsbury and we were walking the two and a half miles from the main road with our purchases. I had shared my mother's disappointment the more keenly because I had the extra burden of a high-tension battery for the wireless in one hand and the accumulator freshly charged and swinging like a solid lead weight in the other. "He's just the same: hail-fellow-well-met. Hope-you've-got-rid-of-your-boil!"

Aunt Alice went off into another roulade and actually *hummed!*

CHAPTER
SEVEN

Growing up Gracefully

We all went to church at Easter (except for Dad) and sang "Jesus Christ is risen today", taking a pole vault over all the high notes. Every time an alleluia came in sight it was an invitation to sing loud. "Christ our passover is sacrificed for us; therefore let us keep the feast," we affirmed with "sincerity and truth". "Christ is risen from the dead; and become the first fruits of them that slept . . . For as in Adam all die; even so in Christ shall all be made alive." It was all good Pauline certitude.

Mr Parrott was in his element, more splendidly chasubled than ever and able to run rings round the Romans and Corinthians. The low-angled sun jigged and jousted through the lancets on to arum lilies that looked like shields of fleur-de-lys. The warrior saints in the stained glass shone: St Michael, St Maurice, St Alban, St Edmund, St George, St Leonard and St Martin. But dimly glimpsed through the siege of Lent, they now blazed cap-à-pie to take the field again in time for Crispin's Day. If a multicoloured palfrey had ridden in on a rainbow no one would have been surprised. The collection was enormous.

158

"A happy Easter! Aren't the daffodils lovely!" People stood around the churchyard after and actually talked. Aunt Alice shook hands with nearly everybody. The church-warden, Farmer B., whispered to me: "A wealthy old woman is that." Steadfast and upright, Aunt Alice dismissed him with a nod. She was dressed for a stay in the country, fur-collared and sensibly shod. She was all in brown: brown shoes, brown coat, brown hat. As she walked down the path I thought of the trumpeting daffodils and the blazoning stained glass. She could have been downright flamboyant. Instead she was upright and plain.

"How old are you, Aunt Alice?" I asked as the evening wore on.

"Ninety-five." She smiled dismissively. She was casting on, or casting off. Sometimes she asked me to hold a hank of wool round my thumbs while she wound it into a ball.

"You shouldn't ask ladies their age." My mother prodded her tooth with a needle, but really she was poking me.

"And how is Nellie Thonger now?" Aunt Alice asked.

"Oh wonderful, considering. She's very blind." My mother's eyes looked miles away and her lips closed tight over the needle.

"And the other Nellie?"

"Nellie Birchall? She's living in a bungalow at Fenemere. She's asked us to go sometime."

"What's a bungalow?" asked Belle. "And where's Fenemere?"

"A place without stairs and near Eyton," my mother crisply replied.

Aunt Alice wondered why we had so many warts. I had several on my hands and John had one on his ear. Did we get them from the beasts? I stopped my shadow play above the fire and Laura tucked her hands away before the old witch noticed her nails and threatened some dire remedy for them.

"You all look healthy enough in other respects." She emphasized the point by wrapping up her knitting and taking up a book. What would it be, I wondered. *Alice in Wonderland*, I bet. More mad tea parties and terrible goings-on at the Red Queen's croquet ground. (Aunt Alice pronounced it "croaky". She read it aloud, a little bit each year. A little was enough.)

"We'm never bad!" said John, expert in defence, and knowing what effect his choice of words would have. She nearly dropped the book.

"Please, please! You're never ill!"

"We're always good," Belle chipped in. "Even when we're ill!"

"Oh come, you've all jumped out of the knife box!"

"Out of the knife box and straight up to bed!" Mother was quick on the uptake too. The old grandfather clock struck nine. "He's murdering the time! Off with his head!"

The following Sunday, and by special dispensation because I was the one and only Little Ness choirboy now, I was given leave to go with Mother and Aunt Alice to evensong at Great Ness church. "It's at

160

three-thirty you know," I said, "because of the blackout." So we set off in good time, Aunt Alice setting the pace. It was dry enough to take the short cut down the old Cow Lane. The oak tree was unfolding its little rusty thumb-sized leaves. The fists of the ash were still clenched tight. A sycamore was red and fully out. You could smell the strong new grass at the base of the hedge. Aunt Alice squeaked and stooped to bless a clump of celandines, which she called "celandeens", and nearly made us late. The birds were singing in the churchyard and the organist was playing Mendelssohn's Song without Words No. 4. I knew because I'd learnt it; and my teacher was the organist. We had a box pew. The stained glass in the afternoon light, the surplices in procession down the aisle, the roly-poly parson, Mr Brighton, with a verger to show him to his place — you might have been in a cathedral, in a cathedral-sized congregation. "The scripture moveth us ..." We confessed our "uncloked sins". "O Lord open Thou our lips." Mr Brighton had a voice to fit his double chins. And where was the organ coming from? All was hid in a distant, dark immensity. And the choir shewed forth its praise: soprano, alto, tenor, bass. In "Ye choirs of new Jerusalem" my mother sang a beautiful alto which in Little Ness church would have sounded odd and almost out of tune. And the choir hauled us into the final Alleluia Amen as an apotheosis. We normally left that out.

Mr Brighton mounted the pulpit beaming cherubically at a daffodil. "Isn't that marvellous!" It was. We had a nature lesson. He told us how God brought all things back to life and lifted them up. After two years a dragonfly nymph rose from the mud at the bottom of a pond into the light to shed its imprisoning wing shields, pump blood into its system, feel the life and colour coming into its wings and zoom off on its honeymoon. I looked at Mother and she snuggled up to me. Mr Brighton left out parts of the life history of my favourite insect, but it was so different from anything I had heard at Little Ness I asked if I could come again. He stood outside and shook hands with us as with long lost friends. "Is this your youngest? Have you learnt to swim?" I had, and Mother said I had enough on my plate anyway.

It was half past four and getting dusk. The sun had sunk behind the Ruddiferns. Five old hens who had stayed out late on the Poplars Field prompted Aunt Alice to chuckle, "The fox will get you!" And, indeed, when we entered the lane the overhanging tunnel made by ivy-tousled hedges was not quite dark. The scent was heavy on the breeze of fox's den and badger's sett.

We passed the old manure heaps — heaving, bubbling, pungent pools all stuffed with straw and stiff with grass. The last of the sunset was reflected in the mullioned windows of Little Ness House before the maids could draw the blinds. We reached home just in time to tune into *The Selfish Giant* on the wheezy old wireless, the new batteries boosting the Hail and the North Wind with what Mother expressively called "juice".

★ ★ ★

"Where there's a hill there's a legend," said Johnny in the afternoon of the day we returned to school for the summer term. "What's in a name?" he asked. "Take, if you like, our own town — Scrobb's Fort, or Scrobbesbury, as it was called. There are innumerable hills: Port Hill, Pride Hill, Swan Hill, College Hill . . ." The names came from the class as well: "Wyle Cop, Dogpole, Castle Hill, Coton Hill . . ."

"Yes, and Saint John's Hill; and all those steep little snickets like Gullet Passage, Roushill, Bear Steps, Grope Lane — you can imagine what went on there — the Pig Trough . . . they all have a story to tell. And then there are the hills beyond the town."

He reminded us of them and the legends associated with them: Pontesford Hill and the Golden Arrow, the Stiperstones and the Devil's Chair, the Long Mountain and Wild Edric, Corndon and the legend of Mitchell's Fold. Finally he gave us the story of the origin of the Wrekin to act out.

The Devil, having a grudge against the mayor and townspeople of Shrewsbury, threatened to dam up the Severn and cause a great flood. Tired with carrying a giant shovelful of earth a very long way, and meeting a cobbler close to Wellington, he told him of his plan. The cobbler had a lot of customers in Shrewsbury so, when the Devil asked him how far it was, he said it was a devil of a, ahem, terrible long way. "Look," he said, showing him the heavy sack he had been carrying on his back, "at all the boots and shoes I've worn out coming from Shrewsbury now!"

163

"Oh," said the Devil, and dropped his earth and turned for home. And the dirt he scraped off his boots was the little hill at Ercall by the Wrekin's side.

"Find out more about your hills and their legends," said Johnny when the bell went. "Act them, draw them, write them. Look beyond the names." He waved an unused piece of chalk. "Start at home tonight."

On my way home on the bus I wondered which I should choose. I knew about Mitchell's Fold where the poor people in a time of drought had come to milk the cow that would always give milk so long as they did not milk her dry; but a witch had come along with a sieve and the cow, milked dry, had gone away and never come back. I knew about Wild Edric who rode his white horse over the Long Mountain on windy, moonlit nights. My mother had a book called *The Golden Arrow* by Mary Webb. But I didn't know enough about any of these. Pushing my bike up Montford Bank and playing a tune by poking pieces of long-stemmed grass in the front-wheel spokes, I suddenly remembered Humphrey Kynaston, the highwayman of Nesscliffe Hill. No one else would think of him! Nobody had mentioned Nesscliffe Hill! I would have it all to myself!

Later that evening, we were all sitting in the cosiness of the sitting-room, the fire striking stars from the soot at the back of the chimney's throat; all, that is, except Dad, who was probably closer to the highwayman than I — at Nesscliffe, sitting in Kynaston's Seat at the Old Three Pigeons' Inn. Mother was darning and dreaming, listening to *Tons of Money* on the wireless. John was a boy on the map of Arabia, plotting his way by our Aladdin lamp. Laura was reading *The Midnight Folk* and Belle *The Secret Garden*. I was trying to draw steps.

"How many steps up to Kynaston's Cave?" I asked wearily.

"Twenty-six?"

"Twenty-four?"

"Twenty-five?"

Answers came from all sides.

"Look it up," Mother said.

"In what, please?" I asked, carefully.

"In Mr Brighton." Mother rose from her seat, gave the fire a poke with her foot and went over to the cupboard full of books.

"He's not been looked at for ages." She dusted his jacket and out dropped a letter:

Dear Mrs Davies,

As you kindly said you would like a copy of *The Story of Great Ness* I am sending same with Olive Watkins.

The cost of printing has been heavy & I am asking people to subscribe not less than three shilling a copy or 7 for £1-0-0.

Hope you have got rid of your boil. Every good wish.

Yours sincerely,
F. Brighton.

"There you are," she said, "Chapter One: 'Nesscliffe Hill'," and left me to get on with it.

165

"Nesscliffe must have been the central battleground of all the struggles in the history of these parts," Mr Brighton said. And then he came to the highwayman. He had stage-managed him well. A brief setting of the scene: Nesscliffe Hill, the iron-age fort, the look-out over the lake that is now the Prill; the lighthorseman rallied with a good horse, sword and spear to warn the sleeping townsmen when the Welshmen would attack. And when the Welsh were conquered, the vacuum was filled with a Watling Street haunted by highway robbers. Enter Humphrey (the local hero) Kynaston!

Mr Brighton settled to writing the "quaint story" transcribed with mutiple "aforesaids" and "feloniously strucks" of a crime and the inquest that followed it. "And the aforesaid Humphrey Kynaston riding upon a horse, with a certain lance, of the worth of twelve pence, in his right hand, rode at the aforesaid John Heughes and feloniously struck him on the right side of his breast, and gave him a deadly blow whereof the said John Heughes then and there died."

According to the account that followed the wild-eyed Humphrey outwitted the sheriff, whose orders were that his men should remove some of the planks from the wooden bridge spanning the Severn at Montford and wait in ambush under the bridge.

Arrived the Wild Humphrey on his trusty horse and leapt clear the treacherous gap.

He had been gatekeeper at Myddle Castle in his youth and, so said Richard Gough in his *History of Myddle*, lived out his days in the cave, pardoned by the King.

What Mr Brighton didn't tell — through the holes in his dry, yellow-flake parchments — my young imagination amply supplied. For Nescliffe Hill was one of our favourite summer hunting grounds. Like lizards on a sun-warmed sandstone wall we flickered round its sides, we wriggled in and out of holes, submerged in rhododendrons, burst blinking into light, and always ended up by the steps — the haunting, hollowed, hoof-marked steps that led us to the cave.

The cave, Mr Brighton said, had been a quarryman's house, approached by a flight of twenty-six steps roughly hewn from the rock. Whole families had lived there in two tiny rooms. How poor they must have been! There was a hole in the roof. A wild gooseberry sprouted there now, but there were still charred embers of a fire on the floor below. The sandstone trough at the bottom of the steps was where the highwayman led his horse, lathered and white-eyed like himself, to drink. What was its name, I wondered. Bess, perhaps. No, Hambletonian, more like.

I had not time to draw the horse or the masked and tricorn-hatted highwayman. It was time for bed. But I could see his shadow on the stairs. His cloak was the curtain which flew out of the attic window as I opened the door and the wind blew my candle out.

Spring came with the lilacs, the lilacs with the spring. Wherever there was an earth closet, there, spiked and heraldic, purple and white, stood the fragrant lilac trees. With what a profusion of scented foam they

167

commanded the sun to stay out! They had an ally in the laburnum, whose pendant blooms dripped liquid gold.

And with the true spring came more visitors. The gypsies, with their clothes-pegs, led the trail. The piano tuner came. He could not leave a note alone, but eventually with a frantic onrush, a petulant clatter of broken chords, moved up a notch and ended with a snatch of G.H. Clutsam's "Lilac Time". And Peggy One-tooth Sambrook, an old friend of my mother's from Nesscliffe, came. Her bottom tooth stuck up and out, as did her nose. She wore a mid-Victorian hat and fox's fur thrown round her neck. It startled me, the way it bit into its own backside. She poked me with a bony claw and said, with ostrich eyes and owlish hoots, "Play, Peter, play."

Violet, who worked next door, showed off to me by jumping the privet hedge. The real spring was a glimpse of a girl's careering underwear.

The tailor came to measure us for suits. "Short trousers still?" he asked with tearful eyes. "And for a long time yet," our mother prophesied.

The cuckoo came. The swallows came. And Topsy, five days after foaling, was visited by Little Spark of Llansantffraid, a little black Jack-in-the-box with foaming mouth and frenzied eye. She squealed at him, he kicked at her, and she kicked back.

Spring now splashed the house with sun and really settled in. Early potatoes were up in the gardens and some people said they had dug "tuthree" (two or three) roots. The Chesney boys had swum in the river. And Mrs Kay at the Herb Farm had grown tomatoes under glass. All rhubarb and rumours! What was certain was that the cows were now doing well and this year's hay was already a good foot high.

And Jim and Lucy came. They were our old neighbours from the Wigmarsh days. They came one Sunday — on such shining bicycles, so upright and well looked after, they made us feel ashamed of our broken-down old crocks. Jim looked like a constable, his mac folded over one shoulder. Lucy stepped down from the seat like a dancer on her points. Setting and balancing, they placed their machines against the wall. Jim took his trouser clips off as if they were tiaras and patted his pocket to make sure they were there. Lucy had flashing eyes, a loud enamelled laugh and long enamelled teeth; but Jim had soft brown eyes which played under the peak of his oatmeal-coloured, soft, flat cap. "Well fancy!" was what he mostly said: a useful, all-purpose response. A new calf, a tide of day-old chicks, our flourishing ferrets, the number of churns on the milk stand ... "Well fancy!" How I had grown. Had we been here ten years? Still got the old Alice cow? "Well fancy!"

It would be a lamb lunch, with or without new potatoes; and we would almost certainly have young rhubarb, pink and sweet. "Well fancy!" And after lunch, and Lucy's laugh and Jim's soft-spoken deference, we'd chew the cud among the cows. Deep in daisies, Jim and Dad and John and I would run our hands along their backs, for cows are as susceptible as cats to gentle massage of their supple vertebrae. They dip voluptuously. This simple, but time-honoured ceremony ended, Jim would say: "Time to go home. Well fancy!" He had his own sleek herd to milk. Sun still splashed the white fold gate with extra brightness; and splashed the lilac Lucy bore away.

They came and went, the softly spoken, gentle Jim and Lucy laughingly.

It was the Whitsun holiday. I had discovered two new nests: a blackie's and a chaffinch's. There were five blackbirds' in the orchard already. They built early. You suddenly realized they were there, complete, prefabricated, whole. But the chaffinch still had a lot more work to do: collecting moss, wool, hair, feathers and grass and decorating the outside with lichen and bits of bark. I planned to watch it for days. And keep it dark.

"Coo-ee! Come on, or we'll be late!" called Mother. How often had I heard that cry! I jumped the hurdle in the hedge and ran like a decoy up the road to make it seem that I had come from another direction.

"Put your coat on. We're going to Fenemere," said Mother — already poised to click her tongue and drive the black pony hell for leather through the lanes, surprising roadmen as we passed and making staid old hunters skip like colts and find their springtime legs again.

Emerging from an avenue of horse chestnuts we entered Baschurch.

"Can we stop at Uncle Percy's shop?"

"On the way back — if there's time. I told Auntie Nellie Birchall we'd stay for tea." I tried to weigh the relative merits of Uncle Percy's sweets and Auntie

Nellie's tea. No doubt about it: it would be nice to have both.

We had never seen a bungalow. Auntie Nellie and Uncle Charlie had had a series of rented homes. Something had gone wildly wrong with their affairs and this was what Mother called a "stopgap". I pictured a gap in the hedge, stopped with thorns — and I was not far wrong. In a field, in the lea of a hedge, complete with the desirable remains of a hay stack, and enclosed with a barbed-wire fence, was Auntie Nellie's bungalow. Duckboards, an improvised veranda and a lean-to for the motor-bike and sidecar gave it, in the early summer, quite a holiday air. But it could not have been much fun in winter. A simple structure of wood and tin or corrugated iron, it was like a pioneer homestead. A plume of smoke from the stovepipe and my aunt waving a tea-towel from the veranda and scattering the free-range hens made the picture complete.

"Eddie's staying with us — he's just gone to meet Charlie."

My aunt's greatest joy was to minister to the needs of her visitors. In more spacious times she had taken paying guests but always called them visitors. And they came year after year as friends to be thoroughly spoilt by her attentive hospitality and farmhouse fare.

To watch Auntie Nellie buttering bread and slowly slicing it was to realize that it was too important to be done in a hurry. Preparation for tea was like preparation for Communion. And she would bring out a cake which you knew had been made with so many

171

eggs that it could be kept like wine, its goodness guaranteed. Her sauces, chutneys and preserves were all from the urtext recipes of Nesscliffe Hotel.

We marvelled too at her home-making skills. Here was this tiny place, not much bigger than a poultry house, so neat and finely furnished inside that the Queen would have been pleased to sit at tea with us. A little poker-work text in wood said "Where your treasure is there will your heart be also".

In came cousin Eddie and Uncle Charlie and we all sat down to tea. The talk was of Aunt Alice, the Easter services at Little Ness and Great Ness, and of course the old, old, happy days. Mention Aunt Alice and Uncle Charlie always said: "Behold the lilies of the field, they toil not neither do they spin . . . But if she was talking to you in the lane and her eye lighted on a ha'penny in the mud she'd leave off her fine and fancy thoughts and grab it — before you could say J.D. Rockefeller."

Eddie and John were about the same age and very soon Auntie Nellie had persuaded Mother that John could stay the night. "We might find a curlew's nest!" said John. They would go looking for newts in the fields crisscrossed by mossy dykes. Uncle Charlie kept a cow as well as free-range hens and we all enjoyed watching him milk and scattering Indian corn from a bowl-dish. We tried to find out what Uncle Charlie did for a living. He said he kept the drains and ditches dry.

After looking at souvenirs of TT races in the Isle of Man, and mementoes of Little Ness and Nesscliffe Hotel, we had time for only one wild leap from the hay stack before harnessing the pony and driving home full tilt.

"We'll just call in at the shop in Baschurch," said Mother; and we were able to twist our Uncle Percy's arm for black-market sweets. Under the avenue of horse chestnuts, to the delightful echoes of the pony's hooves and the reverberant rumble of the well-sprung tub, I was sorely tempted to eat John's share. Belle was artfully persuading Billy that the spare henhouse in the fields at home, appropriately enclosed by a barbed-wire fence, would make a marvellous bungalow. They would raid the quarry for bits of thrown-out china and invite their friends to tea. My sister had saved the wrappers off the buns from tea and, with a few imaginative texts and a collage of egg shells inscribed "A present from the Isle of Man", they would set up home like Auntie Nell. "You'll have to go out to work of course," she said — and took his sweets, "to keep them safe."

CHAPTER
EIGHT

Our New, Expanding Universe

Billy went back to Liverpool in early June, almost as unexpectedly as he had arrived. That was the way with evacuees. Those sharing the Priory had also decamped. We, the regular tenants, returned to ruling newer, fuller timetables at school. There was more time now to tabulate.

As spring warmed into summer, boys from Shrewsbury came as far afield as Little Ness. They came to see if what they'd heard was true. Along the little sandstone wall the boys propped up their bikes, drop handle-barred, derailleur-geared, too good to mix with our entanglements we tumbled in the shed. All older boys, they were John's friends. He showed them how he tucked his ferrets in his shirt. They came, they saw and went away.

The first of my friends to come was Maurice More. He startled even Mother by the intensity of his attack on Mr Waggs, his bus and his whole company. Had Maurice lost his ticket? Had he been asked to pay twice? Had someone doubted his word? We could not

174

tell. Maurice, as a young socialist, had a strong sense of justice and the vocabulary — but not on this occasion the coherence — to match.

Mother liked him from the start. Smart he was, she said. He came on the second Saturday in June in long grey flannels whose creases looked naive, to say the least. "How nice to see a tie," she sang — and might have added, fitting collar, jacket, handkerchief and cuffs (all clean) and polished shoes.

Maurice was the son of the Co-op butcher, the eldest of umpteen children, all endowed with bright eyes, clear skins and teeth like peeled almonds. He had a firm mouth, confident chin, and eyes that burned darkly, daringly sometimes. For Maurice had a mission. He wanted to see World's End. I looked at his shoes. We could not walk. My bicycle had a puncture. John was using his. Those of the girls were too small.

We went on Topsy (quite used to carrying two), and called at the post office for sweets.

"A pennyworth of winegums, please." I had instructed Maurice so well that he came out of the post office with not one extra winegum but two. And a lump of sugar for the pony. Mrs Garry had heard her scrunching around outside and seen me craning my neck and mouthing to Maurice through the window: Winegums, pleease.

"Players please, as well," said he, flashing a packet of ten.

"Howja get them?" I asked.

"For Mr Davies, I said."

"For Mr More, more like," said I. "Mr Davies always has Woodbines. And Mrs Davies has hers on account."

Maurice was now faced with the problem of getting on the pony behind me without a sandstone wall or other handy mounting block.

"I tell you what," I said. "I'll get off and leg you up and then I'll leap-frog on behind you." Which I did, taking the reins and navigating blind. All I knew was that the winegums were going down as Maurice hollered fruity observations which gusted over his shoulder as Topsy broke into a staccato trot. The lane past the church led to the Bottom Buildings. Hedges drowned in cow parsley. We passed a field of beans in flower . . . The cuckoo hiccupped and went on . . . Three men and a woman, bent over hoes, were singling beet.

"Behold her single in the field," said Maurice, after I had explained that singling meant leaving only one out of three plants to grow.

"They're doing piecework," I said. "They might do an acre a day. Or more. A man can plough an acre a day. But hoeing's real backbreaking work."

"Who owns these fields?" asked Maurice.

"My uncle," I said.

"Plutocrat," said he.

We passed the shepherd leaning on his Foxholes gate, his trousers open with a wide V in front, in spite of a strong leather belt.

"Pastoral *embonpoint*," said Maurice.

"Ay, shepherds are kings," I shouted, "hereabouts. No piecework for them."

176

"Who works hardest then?" asked Maurice.

"Jack Whiteside, I should think. A little chap. Eight or ten children. Thirty shillings a week . . ." We passed his wife, who was twice his size, big-buttoned and booted and bouncing with her baskets from the bus stop at a jig. "You won't see another human being till we reach Platt Mill," I said. "Have a smoke now and save the winegums till later, to sweeten your breath."

And on we went from World's End with its twin cottages, its wind-puffed cockerels and shrinking hens, its struggling clotheslines strained with billowing shirts and dancing pinafores, on down towards Platt Mill. I had told him about the workmen's homesteads of the Bottom Buildings, the Foxholes and this, the last outpost to the north before Ruyton-XI-Towns; where the fields sloped down to the Perry, where it was so peaceful in the sunshine that you might even see an otter asleep.

A heron lifted off ponderously. "What's that? An albatross?"

"No, a heron. A couple of pounds of flying frogs' legs. All feathers and skin. And thinner bones than mine," I added, adjusting my terminus on Topsy's rump. And then John, the waggoner's lad, emerged from the alders by the bank. "Why aren't you singling?" I said.

"I'm just doing a nice bit of trout tickling before I goes to see to the mares and foals. No singling for me."

John's adam's apple bobbed in his throat as he inhaled from one of Maurice's proffered cigarettes; his eyes half closed.

"Have one," he said to me, indicating that Maurice had plenty left. We hitched the pony to a thorn bush and John led us to a shady hollow where a silver trout lay wide-eyed, startled on the bank. "You know there's a fish where there's a heron," he said. "I seed an otter too."

We sat and smoked, squatting under the trees, still as the boulders that shrouded the fish, keeping our thoughts to ourselves, sheltered from the breeze, in a ring of fragrant fire.

"I won't get another fish," John said. "Not now." He slapped his thighs.

"D'you know what time it is?" We none of us had a watch.

"It's milking time," said John. "It's three o'clock."

"We haven't had our lunch," I said. "There's a lad here with one small fish," I said to Maurice, not very persuasively.

"We'll have a winegum each," he said. And to us, his smoky-tonsilled comrades, he was our sweet-toothed king.

Apart from Maurice's best trousers, which had lined themselves with Topsy's hairs — more white than grey — we did not think we presented too bad a picture when we got home.

"Your dinner's on the table," Mother said. "Cold rabbit pie and bread — and not much butter. We waited till two o'clock."

My two sisters sat round the table with us, drawn it seemed by some sense of awe. How had Maurice conquered Mother's pride? It was then that he, normally so poised and sensible, breathed. When he shouldn't have done.

"You've been smoking," Laura exclaimed.

Maurice said nothing.

"What did you say, Laura?" Mother glared.

"Nothing."

"No one ever says nothing."

"I never said nothing." We slipped easily into the vernacular, especially when we wished to strengthen our denials — I aren't, I weren't, we wosn't — in the face of such exactitude.

"Ol' man river, dat ol' man river," Maurice sang to his fork, "he must know sumpin, but don't say nothing', he just keeps rollin', he keeps on rollin' along."

He was stepping dangerously round the iced edges of Mother's sensibility. She drew in her breath and hacked a doorstep off the shipwrecked loaf. "If you want any more you can cut it yourselves." We were not normally allowed to touch the knife.

"Cerebos salt is made from bones," Maurice spontaneously announced.

"Shut up," said Mother, "and get on with your dinner!"

"Perfume is made from the anal gland . . ." (My blossoming sisters, all attar of roses, probably prompted this.) Slap! went my mother's hand round Maurice's startled trap.

Maurice and Mother always got on after that. She still thought he was smart. "He'll end up", she said, "with an attaché case, a rolled umbrella and a bowler hat."

I had neglected my music of late; but that June I began to take lessons in town. Gone were the happy-go-lucky days of pony rides and gate-crashing Rachmaninoff. So was the caraway seedcake. I went to Miss Oppenheimer who taught at Mrs Wynne Corrie's house in College Hill. I went on Wednesdays after school and played on a Broadwood grand. I began to learn the Forty-eight Preludes and Fugues by Bach.

Mrs Corrie's house was open to many musicians, some very well known at the time. Mr F.C. Morris came and partnered her in the "Golden Sonata" by Purcell. Alfred Cave, another violinist, heard me play a Bach prelude and told me to give it more spit. "You can polish it later," he said. Someone sang "One Fine Day" and nearly blew me out of the room. But none of Mrs Corrie's friends was more delightful than Miss Oppenheimer. She opened my eyes and ears by her marvellous playing of Beethoven and Mozart sonatas. And, knowing the importance of having an audience (as well as being one), she gave us, her pupils, a chance to perform in public too.

The boy whose lesson followed mine was Robert Walton. He partnered me in the Fingal's Cave Overture, or "the He Brides" as we preferred to say. I played secondo, relishing the rolling of the sea and sustaining the pedal longer than advised. Miss Oppenheimer drew little sheep all over the page followed by stars which represented pedal and release.

180

But with such a sea running, so many storms brewing and Robert's turbulent treble coming down on me, I flattened my foot, somehow thinking I was holding the storm-lashed wreckage together.

"You can play it in our musical evening on Friday night," Miss Oppenheimer said.

"I can't get home," I spluttered out.

"You can stay the night with me," kind Robert said.

"Thanks," said I and, almost forgetting my music, rushed down Roushill for the five o'clock bus to Montford Bridge, then cycled home.

It was all fixed up. I could go to Alwyn's for tea after school on Friday, then to Mrs Corrie's for the performance, spend the night with Robert and go home on Saturday. I could not wait for Friday afternoon to come. I had just Thursday night to get myself prepared. Mother would lend me her small attaché case and pack my clean pyjamas, checking that my underwear was "as it should be if you had to go to hospital". I shut myself up in the Empty Room and practised the piano till my arms fell off. Scales ascending, scales descending, scales in contrary motion and in thirds: I played them all, and, making up for months of idleness, I saw the daylight out.

"It's not the number of notes you play that matters," Mother said, "but the way you play each note", and pushed me off to bed.

On Friday after school I went with my best friend Alwyn to his house in Monkmoor Road. I had never been in a townhouse before. They had electric light, a bathroom (flush lavatory) and a style about the place, so clean and sweet, I was almost afraid to eat my tea. I might cough or have to blow my nose . . . I didn't want to lick my fingers but I didn't want to use the folded serviette. I was most careful how I stirred my tea and how I held my cup.

Alwyn had a wind-up gramophone and some records of Kreisler and Caruso, all with a picture of a dog turning his ear to the horn. His mother told me that as a little boy Alwyn would only listen to HMV records. He liked to stand on a stool and watch the dog and the words "His Master's Voice" go round.

I had time to hear only "Vesti la giubba" before going to join Robert and the other performers at Mrs Corrie's house. We sat nervously listening to many items, vocal and instrumental, before eventually Robert and I rowed into Fingal's Cave, but so much more genteelly now. Small busts of Handel and Bach, Mozart and Beethoven, looked down reprovingly. Mrs Corrie looped her necklace through her elegant but agitated hands. Hands do act as dampers and my foot had lost its ancient power.

Then home with Robert to his palace in Belle Vue. I only remember the carpets, the huge mirrored wardrobe and the lampshades everywhere adding richness and colour and light to things that were already beyond my dreams.

I sank unslippered into the deep-piled bedroom carpets. I switched on lights, nervously hoping my pyjamas were clean and my worn-out toothbrush would not be noticed in the traffic to the bathroom. I wanted to wallow in the turquoise bath with its Oil of Ulay displayed and odours of Edom and offerings divine. But I had to brush my teeth without spotting the mirror and I was nervous about splashing water anywhere.

I smuggled my blackened toenails under the spotless sheets. I watched Robert tidying his clothes and composing himself for the night, not directly but through the full-length mirror on the wardrobe. It seemed to add to his elegance. His black hair seemed blacker, his long back broader and his olive-brown torso more olive-brown where mine was pinched and white. He smiled at me in the mirror and I felt ashamed. I turned over. No one would stand around in our house with nothing on like that!

Excitement ran high the following Tuesday at school. In the afternoon we cricketers — the Colts, we proudly called ourselves — were playing house matches: Sabrina v. St Austin's, Priory v. Stafford. Tim and I were in Sabrina House; Alwyn and Maurice in St Austin's. A civil war between four musketeers.

Lunch that day was a scramble of pointed knives and unchewed mouthfuls of meat which someone said was heart. "Kite's reading *Dracula*," Maurice said. Then we all wanted to know what Kite wouldn't tell.

"Do they get him in the end?"

"Who, the Count? Don't know. Haven't got there yet."

"Where did you get the book?"

"Not telling you."

Maurice and Alwyn didn't know. They wouldn't have been allowed to have it in the house. It wasn't in the school library whose shelves were lined with Percy F. Westerman, Jeffery Farnoll and Rafael Sabatini. And it wasn't in the public library. So where had Kite got it from? Whatever the answer, he was well versed in it. He teased us between big mouthfuls of steamed pudding. "I have give you all information is possible. Please ask no question more. Forgive me if I pain. This so lovely lady, un-Dead in that lonely churchyard — the sacred bell tolling 'Toll! toll! toll!'"

We played cricket at Longden Road, a long way out of town. Maurice and Alwyn went on their bikes. Tim, rather luckily, walked with me: over the Pengwern suspension bridge, along the riverside path by Shrewsbury school, the boathouse, toll bridge, cinder path, then up by Luciefelde Road across the bypass on to Longden Road. Tim never hurried anyway, and now — house match or no house match — his meditative pace quite suited me.

"Well, why couldn't they just leave the lady in her marble house and get off after the Count?" I asked as we crossed the river.

He sidestepped from the point, however, the peak of his cap drawn deep down over his grey reflective eyes. "You're a dark horse," I twitted him. Indeed Tim walked just like a classy horse, up on his toes, and not quite straight.

"Ah," he said when we reached the boathouse and we had to go in single file, "she wasn't in the tomb that night. She was transformed into the Stabbing Woman or the Woman in Black, you see. She hadn't been garlicked then."

"What *do* you mean?" I asked, toiling up the steps by the toll bridge leading to the cinder path. He explained that she would only stay in the tomb after a stake had been driven through her heart and garlic thrust down her throat.

We were fielding in the deep — St Austin's having won the toss — before he told me how Jonathan Harvey went to Count Dracula's castle in Transylvania and how he found in the ruined chapel fifty great wooden boxes filled with fresh earth. Here Tim scooped up a mole hill and ran the earth sensuously through his long elegant hands.

"And the Count was in one?"

"Yes, but he escaped at night and shipped the boxes to Whitby. After killing the crew, he came ashore as a wolf. He set up in Essex, next to a lunatic asylum."

"And that's where he got this so lovely lady?"

"Yes, Lucy. Dr Seward, the head of the asylum, and van Helsing pump blood into her the way they pump gas into an Oldsmobile. In vain. She dies — but remains un-Dead until staked through the heart."

We abstracted ourselves from the game, beyond the range of most of the batsmen's shots. We chewed grass. Kite even lay down, ruminating on garlic and other matters of life and death. Once, with supple urgency, I leapt at what I thought was the ball soaring over my head, but it was really a sparrow. Then one of Alwyn's well-timed glances to fine-leg sent us scurrying to retrieve the ball and the honour of the side.

Dukes, our captain, rearranged his field and I lost contact with the Count for the remainder of the game. Padded up in the pavilion for what was to be a fruitless innings for us, we were much too un-private to talk of Dracula.

Alwyn was known to everybody as Dickie. Even his father called him Dickie. He was a special sort of boy; the product of a good home where Christ was proclaimed "the head of this house, the unseen guest at every meal, the silent listener to every conversation . . .". His parents were extremely proud of him. He was a credit to their trust.

Good-looking and animated, he was always doing something with his hands; boring into the palm of one with the index finger of the other; rapidly propelling the fourth finger inwards while the thumb propelled itself away from the rest of the hand; drawing the tips of his fingers down his cheeks where the hair was beginning to put a shine on his face before turning to a shadow; and endlessly dismissing a wavy black quiff which played over his forehead, teasing it back into place. He had eyes which probably twinkled in his sleep. Good-naturedly. Open, they were richly good-humoured with a depth of benevolence.

I knew my sister Belle had looked at him. I thought my mother would approve of him. I hoped my father would not swear.

After tea on the Friday evening that Alwyn came to stay, I took him up to the attic. Splendidly redecorated for the summer, it was now more "home" for me than anywhere else in the house. In it I kept my books: *Black Beauty*, of course, *The Observer's Book of Birds* and *The Observer's Book of Birds' Eggs*. And my village book.

"I see," said Alwyn. "*Birds* and *Birds' Eggs*."

"Yes, I can show you a kestrel's." I kept my collection in a box near my bed. So we sat on the bed sorting them out.

"Oh, they're magnificent," he said. And they were — all packed in fresh cotton-wool, with only the crack in the kestrel's to dent my pride.

"What's this one?" Alwyn pointed to one near the kestrel's.

"That's a lapwing's."

"It's more pointed."

"Yes, we get plenty of them. We have them for breakfast."

"Never! You don't mean to tell me you eat those beautiful birds' eggs!"

"Those, and those, and those . . ." I pointed to the moorhen's and the coot's.

"You rotter!" He was laughing. His white teeth and fresh breath reassured me. I put the box of eggs away before he attacked me on the bed, tickling me and shouting "You rotter!" in mock fury.

It was quite light when we went upstairs but now it grew suddenly dark. A flash of lightning was followed by a roll of thunder.

"Alas the storm is come again: my best way is to creep under his gaberdine . . ." We had been reading *The Tempest* at school. "There is no other shelter

187

hereabout: misery acquaints a man with strange bed-fellows!" We shrouded till the dregs of the storm were past.

At first light Alwyn was studying the form of the long-tailed tit. "And that little thing lays nineteen eggs in a nest of spiders' webs, hair, lichen, moss — and lined with two thousand feathers! I don't believe it!"

"Then you'll have to take it on trust. But I'll show you a nest, before breakfast."

"Before breakfast!"

"Yes, we've got to get some coots' eggs from the marl pit and there's one on the way. Cheerio!"

Half-dressed, I hurtled down the old wooden stairs and out into the rain-fresh fields. June roses had tears on their petals and there were diamonds on the spread leaves and seeded heads of grass. Alwyn had time to dress correctly and catch me up before we reached the parson's field where we found the nest: what Mary Webb in *Precious Bane* might have called a "tossy ball", a dome moulded and crimped with lichen like a fairy's wedding hat, hung in a thicket of may with sloe and bramble intertwined. Where Jimmy would have rushed in like a pachyderm, Alwyn stood back in awe.

The marl pit was a good two fields away but Alwyn could outrun me over a distance, and, from a quick study of the form book, had spotted a coot's nest before I came panting to the edge of the pool. I had wellingtons so I had to wade into the reeds. Coots' nests are accessible enough, with their six, ten, thirteen (or even more) eggs laid out invitingly on the decks of bulky reed barges, moored where the water is shallow but the mud is deep.

Presently the black waters clouded brick red. One wellington stuck and a sockless foot waved in weary detachment over the angry marl. Leave the boot, I told myself. I had to get the eggs.

Of course my feet were wet, of course my socks were wet and my wellingtons would not dry in twenty-four hours. But Alwyn saved me from a hiding over breakfast and we ate the eggs with subdued pleasure, the novelty of it all reflected in the quick glances which did duty for conversation between my sister, Alwyn and me.

Without saying anything, I was determined to show Alwyn a wild duck's nest. We couldn't go before milking, so that meant after tea. The sun was sinking, setting alight the windows of old Lizzie's cottage on The Shruggs. The nest lay the far side of the pool above the waterline at the root of an old hawthorn tree. But you couldn't get at it from the landward side. It was most cunningly concealed. You had to step along a fallen branch of alder lying to one side.

I went sidestepping along the log until I could just see the eye of the duck in the all-enveloping dark. "She's on the nest!"

"Let me see!"

"All right." I side-shuffled back and let Alwyn take a look.

"Isn't that wonderful! Leave her alone."

You couldn't argue with Alwyn. "When they leave the nest they cover the eggs with down from their breast," I said, know-all like, as we went on round the edge of the pit.

"There's one!" A drake rose showing his rings and bands, purple speculum and white fan-tail feathers.

"What's that?" asked Alwyn.

"That's the drake . . . And there's the duck! We've got another nest here!"

Edging our way through the rushes I could see a likely hole above the base of a leaning oak. The roots spread drily about the bank and provided handholds but no place to put my feet. Into the water I went, keeping a grip and hoping the mud would not suck me down. I found the nest, eggs uncovered, and realized that Alwyn was at my elbow. "Keep hold of the tree. There's a boulder we can climb on to."

Alwyn looked in: "One, two, three . . . goodness, however many eggs! I see what you mean about down."

I stretched out a hand to help him on to the rock. Then splash! I lost my footing and we were both in the water.

"Shucks!" he said, shaking his hands to add to the force of the expression.

We beat it back over the Thirty Acres just as it was getting dark. "You won't be able to go home tomorrow in those clothes. You'll have to stay," said I.

"I will," said he. Did that mean he would — or would not?

"Leave those wellingtons outside!" My mother was ready at the door. "You'd better both get in the bath.

190

And then straight to bed." I got the tin bath down from its nail on the wall by the mangle. "You put your things on the back boiler — not next to the tablecloths and sheets! I'll put Alwyn's shirt to soak. Then I'm going out."

I shepherded Alwyn to the screen by the kitchen range. "You'd better sit on those old newspapers," I said. I poured hot water from the small boiler by the fire, adding cold from the bucket behind the screen. Alwyn demurred but went first. "I'll have to throw the dirty water out," I said. I pulled the screen round so that he would not be nervous of my sister and me.

My mottled calves were ringed round with red where my wellingtons had chafed my legs. My scratched thighs were like sandpaper on which a score of matches had been struck.

Alwyn took a long time soaping his hands. I counted the vertebrae in his back. Then, briskly into action, he was out, leaving the water surprisingly warm. There was no more clean for me.

When we had finished we said "Good night", passing Alwyn's shirt steaming over the fireguard in the other room. Belle said she'd do the ironing. Gladly.

There had been a good crop of hay and an easy harvest that year. We did not go to Rhyl "because of the war". But we were not to be confined. While Maurice, Tim and Alwyn were advancing in aircraft recognition, I was still adding to my egg collection and travelling further afield on my pony. The long light days of summer made weekends seem like holidays.

I set off one Friday evening for my Uncle Dick's at Osmarston. South the road led to Montford Bridge, the A5 and, through Preston Montford, to the Welshpool road. The Pavement Gates advertised itself as PRHA (a member of the Public Road Houses Association, I supposed); the drives to private houses were "concealed". Here gardens blossomed trim and neat with archways overhead and the road rang like metal under Topsy's stepping feet. Past Wood End, the turn opposite Rowton Castle led to my uncle's farm, a lane of ruts beset with ponds and quagmires of manure. My knees bled from jutting brambles — but that was nothing to the bug bites I got that night in bed.

And during the day I exchanged a harvest field of modest acreage for one of prairie size; a herd of moderate milking cows for one of higher yields. Here one worked as hard as two and two as hard as four; the girls (Audrey included) were as good as boys and boys as good as men. There was no such thing as play, not now. Only work: harvesting, cutting thistles, catching rabbits, feeding pigs, milking, mucking out — in that or any order, or simultaneously if you could!

The place was overrun by skinny cats and well-fed ferrets by which my cousin Richard sustained his principal industry, rabbit-catching. His was a world of rabbit traps and rabbit skins, of their bowels and their blood.

It was no use complaining about bugs in the bed. No one heard you if you did. You had to fight for sleep. No prayers here — but a ritual wrestling match to lay you out.

Practical jokes were not unknown. You might be surprised in the morning with an untimely but well-aimed, used chamber pot. If after that you felt aggrieved, as I did . . . too bad. You went home for a rest.

The next weekend I went to Sleap. There, my Auntie Gladys's farm had recently been encompassed by an aerodrome. I had to go a roundabout way from Baschurch and Myddle by way of Bilmarsh and the "Burma Road".

"Look what the wind's blown in! How are you then?" The chaffy smiles broke out. "Well, after all those miles, we couldn't send you back!" Topsy, sweating heavily, was soon unsaddled, given a drink, and before I could slip the bridle off she was grazing in the Patch.

Down to business. Hens sitting on goose eggs had to be lifted off for feeding and the eggs turned. Water had to be wheeled out in churns to poultry houses half a mile across a field. We collected hundreds of eggs in a dozen buckets. It was time to mend the fences to keep the cattle out. And burl the sheep.

While my cousin Lily brought in the washing, my aunt broomed down the yard or attended to the incubator, or the "gullies" (goslings) or the "gillanies" (guinea fowl).

Milking time. More buckets and churns. And a cooler. And a Simplex milking machine making a noise, now like a sucking pig, now like a balloon going down. Cousin Norman, using one hand to turn the switch above his head, reached down with the other to haul up a unit on the floor by his feet. Cows clumsily got in the way, occasionally kicking off the cups. "You silly old so and so!" And the bull stood back with his long heels in the channel taking no part, *pro tempore*.

Down to Tilley and Wem Mills. The pony's tap-dance rhythms rang on the concrete Burma Road and the tub made hiccups over the expansion gaps. Singing, Norman brought back bumper bags of bran.

"So now we'll have tea . . ." No, Granddad had no beer. We pedalled off on bikes to fetch Wem Ales.

At last we settled for the night, playing cards or listening to my aunt sing "The Bells of Saint Mary's" in a voice like the choirboy of the year. A Czech airman with an impossible name played Dvorak's *Humoreske* and a Beethoven sonata and accompanied my aunt with a cigarette between two fingers of the left hand . . .

We didn't know that our blacked-out world inside its perimeter road, swooned over by searchlights and planes landing and taking off, was a nerve centre in a five-year war. The planes and the searchlights kept us safe — a little lark's nest on the ground.

The work was hard, the food and company good. And Auntie Gladys, gliding by, her keys in her hand, made sure that all went by the clock. That was her role, to regulate and set the scene: a scene that I was loth to leave and homeward go and take my wages.

The following week I was back on the heather-clad magnetic Cliffe. This was for me the home of the gypsies who, for all I knew, might drive their flat carts laden with great chests, their horses galloping, racing for the sunset over the Breiddens, my Carpathians. They exercised a power of attraction and awe over me. I was drawn to them; I was repelled by them. But I got to know them, one side of them — the daylight side — at least. That Saturday evening I took my brother's whippet Gyp with me, hoping to meet up with the boys, dark-eyed and handsome, and their dogs.

You could sight them through the heather, on a well-worn grassy knoll. Gypsies. Watching. A cloud of patchy horses. Coloured caravans. Blue drift of campfire smoke. Liquid curlicues on vans; the vine-leaf traceries; concave curves and convex curves — a natural geometry. Sepia-grey ancients. Black waistcoats. Spanish hats. Tall womenfolk with ink-black hair, bold rings and shawls. A line of children's washing, red, blue, green. The ever-watchful dogs.

Gypsies watching horses grazing; young ones lazing on the sun-lit earth. Lean, long-legged youths in broad leather belts, brass buckles and studs, stretched out, chewing grass. Keeping a tally. Casting an eye on the width of the world.

Presently two boys surprised me from behind. I knew the taller one as Hiram from our forays into cornfields round the Cliffe. Jimmy knew them too; but his mother called them "didekis" and wouldn't let him play with them.

Hiram, though tall, was shy, with sloe-black hair and eyes and startling teeth. He nudged his brother. "Go on, Ed," he said. And then together they voiced their invitation: "Come wiv we."

195

Hiram had a dog that would catch a hare. "Any dye," he said. Of all the dogs I'd seen, Spike looked the one most likely to catch a hare on open ground. High in the back but short in the foreleg, Spike had a clean, eager mouth and the eye of a small dragon. His ears were like fritillaries. His whole body was sheathed in a kind of velvet snakeskin. He was black with a white "spike" on his front. Like all the gypsy dogs, he never made a sound.

"'E ketched two the other dye." Hiram and Eddie and I strode through the running grasses, silvered with the wind and touched with the blue of a cloudless sky — the "glassy sea" of the hymn. Suddenly a hare came hurtling straight at us.

"'E canna sight us!" Hiram hissed. "The dawg's takin' it aisy."

The hare was weaving, looping, bending, confusing the dog. Just as Spike got to within a foot of him he would jink the other way. Spike could not get a line on him. Once he closed on his rump but a dog can't catch a hare by the tail. I kept tight hold of Gyp.

"'E'll tire 'im. 'E's on'y feintin'," Eddie said. Then the hare suddenly faulted. The dog came on him sideways, closing on the loins, and delivered him straight to Hiram's hand: a sandy beauty nearly three feet long. Defiance burning in his side-set eyes.

"Come wiv we," they said again, after they had hung the hare up in the van. "Us wants to showd yer. See that kerchief on the ground? Watch us on the piebald!" Hiram took a nearby horse called Prince, bridled him and rode in a loop round a line of larch, back by some gorse and on to the level stretch that led back to the camp. There the spotted handkerchief lay on the ground. As Prince came thundering up Hiram reached down and picked it up.

"'Av a go, mistah," said a woman who I took to be his mum.

"Put it on the brash fust," said Eddie, who was more my size. He put it on some sprigs of gorse.

I got on Prince's back (no saddle) and jogged off round the hill. I took a good run at it. I knew what to do. Prince didn't need a bridle. All you had to do was grab his mane, which was nearly as long as his tail, with one hand and hold on tight. Then with the free hand you could reach the handkerchief. If you didn't lose your legs . . . So I stuck my nearside toe practically under Prince's leg and the heel on the other side I dug in as hard as murder on his back.

"An aisy job," said Hiram — his way of congratulating me on my success. And I said all credit was due to Prince. Topsy would have tipped me off.

"Now for rabbits!" Hezekiah, the head of the tribe, came out, with his smoky smell and his belly full of hedgehog, not quite buttoned up. "Come wiv we." We joined him with the lurchers, Nell and Tiny, Nip and Patch; Gyp and Spike romped with them, nudging, bounding over bracken and the sun-bright, brittle grass.

No one spoke; the dogs were silent, gay as we were, free as air. And the rabbits ran to cover on their little bouncy feet. Then a squeal, and you knew you'd got one. Hiram had the most with Spike; but Gyp picked up a couple and I was glad.

Dogs were looking up and laughing, pleased as we were at the catch. Dew was falling and the pine trees smelt like fresh carbolic soap. Here, on the plantation side of the camp, the horses rested in the last rays of the evening sun: the pied mares and the quick-eyed foals at foot. Hiram called them Queenie, Lady and Flower ("Flah" of course). He clicked his tongue and lured a shy foal with his lips. "I'll showd yer summat else," he said. Taking something from his pocket, he held a clenched hand over Lady's withers, moving it slowly over and over her back. At the same time with the other hand he squeezed a jet of milk from her udder.

I had never been allowed to touch Topsy's undersides. Tighten her girth, crawl under her belly — yes. But no more. Yet I had always wanted to touch the comely chalice, ebonized, as sleek as the skin of a seal.

Hiram, still moving his left hand over her back, eyed me to approach. With a lick of his own anointed lips he directed an arc of milk at me. Amazingly I caught it. Instinctively. Opening my mouth at the right moment.

It was toasty, like the oil that I sucked from my fingers when my mum put too much butter on toast.

Nearly forgetting my rabbits, I hurried home across the fields. I tripped over an old hurdle, partly buried in the ground. My shin sang. And when I got home I couldn't peel off my sock. Mother bathed it for me. Looking up she said, "Where have you been? You smell of smoke!" She looked at my face. Putting her finger in her handkerchief, I thought she was going to screw it in my ear. This time she lightly dusted the region of my right temple. "Standing with your mouth open, I'll be bound!"

But I still had a slight smear, a seal as it were, over my right eye.

The summer was dry, the fields full of toxic, gleaming ragwort and brilliant, bitter buttercups. Pasture was scanty and the pit was nearly dry, but not — thank God — the well. Our faithful pump, though gasping sometimes, spluttered on. To a Spitfire pilot under a sapphire sky our village must have looked like a bowl of cream. To the German who landed his Messerschmitt 109 in a sunny field near the Ruddiferns it may have seemed that here was peace with plenty crowned. But the thread of life was thin.

Once when I looked out at night I saw the sun go down, a red, round ball of fire behind the hills. In front of it, the pointed finger that was Rodney's Pillar, stark and black, seemed ominously close. Our world, I knew, was changing. Not only that, but our horizons — or our perception of them — had already changed.

And we were growing apart. John had his friends and I had mine. The eighteen or nineteen months that hardly separated us when I was eleven now seemed like eighteen or nineteen years. I no longer tried to keep up.

Belle and Laura became young ladies and shared with Mother her women's magazines and sighed for a house with a tap.

I seemed, for a short time, to grow closer to my father, to my roots, and the world of hand-milking and horses: that goodly heritage in which my lot was cast.

199

I was glad I had kept my village book. Only once did I bring it out of the attic, and that was to show it to my father.

"Sandstone gravestones lean and lurch
Round the little sandstone church."

He read it aloud, tracing with his finger the artless lines I had written about our sandstone-dominated world.

He traced in the same deliberate way the fields on my map, his tongue dwelling on their evocative names: Rushy Meadow, Banky Meadow, the Vipers Hills, The Legs ... His attention was most drawn to the Red House and the quarry that had provided stone for so much of the building around. He knew exactly how many tons had gone into Adcote Hall.

After the quarry I had put in a little piece which I never intended anyone to see:

The quarry with its gloomy cave
No terror for me bears,
But who can pass — not I alas —
The dungeon by the stairs!

This was accompanied by a shadowy sketch of the cellar door and me going up to bed.

"Who is this little boy?" my father asked, it seemed sympathetically. I hesitated to say. "I had the same fear myself," he said, "when I was young. I still have it. There's nothing worse than the dark — the darkness of a wood in no-man's-land . . ." His mind slipped back to the war. I tried to imagine what it must be like never to hear a siren, or an owl hoot, without being reminded of the shrill whistle of shells, the eerie light of tracer bullets whizzing overhead . . .

"While there's a lucifer to light your fag," he crooned, "smile, boys, that's the style . . . Old soldiers never die, they simply fa-de away."

The day before the end of term Whisky Johnny, clean-shaven, appeared in a new serge suit. Somebody said he had got married. But next morning in assembly the head-master announced that he, along with others of the staff, had volunteered for a great and honourable adventure.

The war had hardly touched our lives at any point. Through the year we had carried our gas masks in cardboard boxes falling to bits and, more permanently, in dark cylindrical tins. One of John's friends had an Anderson shelter in Armoury Gardens near the barracks. I went to play in it. It was more friendly than our cellar — but hardly as profound. And I doubt if Tim had an air-raid shelter in Featherbed Lane.

As for Johnny, he never mentioned such things; and we never saw him again. But in the fourth year our form master received a letter from him in which he said he was dabbling his toes in the Straits of Messina.

Alwyn, Maurice and Tim never did meet Jimmy Roberts. He lived in the twilight, on the edge of a vanishing world. Almost a flat-earther. Tim, Maurice and Alwyn had done things that Jimmy and the gypsies would never do. And they, the guerrillas of the Cliffe, had done things that my town friends would never believe.

I was free to do anything and everything. I had gone with the Ancient Mariner. I had rowed into Fingal's Cave on a Broadwood grand. Tremulous with care, I had held a long-tailed tit's egg double-handed just in case the wind should blow it away, never having felt such pleasure in so small and plain a thing before. I had a kestrel's egg (cracked) in my collection. I had eaten locusts and wild honey. And I had drunk mare's milk.

Also available in ISIS Large Print:

Blackmore Vale Childhood

Hilary Townsend

Now my peace and solitude were about to be threatened much more seriously, for I was five years old and it was time to go to school.

Hilary Townsend was born in the Blackmore Vale and this account of her childhood evokes a way of life that has vanished without trace. Her memories are sharply observed, breathing life into her descriptions of the Vale and the small town of Stalbridge, then the centre of her world.

It was a remote place where change was slow and the agricultural depression meant hard times for almost everyone. Yet the author's delight in the simplest of pleasures, and her boundless interest in everything around her gives this account of growing up in the 1930s its freshness and appeal.

ISBN 978-0-7531-9438-6 (hb)
ISBN 978-0-7531-9439-3 (pb)

Dreams of Hope

Lily O'Connor

From the author of *Can Lily O'Shea Come Out to Play?*

I watched him. He led the floor with the best dancers, the girls who knew his every step.

This sparkling memoir is a remarkable personal account of the emigrant lives of one Irish couple amongst the hundreds upon thousands forced to emigrate in the 1950s.

The book centres on Lily O'Connor's married life with Paddy in Dublin, Luton and Australia. At its heart is the story of a man who always wanted too much and a woman whose resilience saw her coping courageously, often on her own, with a large family and difficult circumstances. This is a resonant tale of one woman's life in three countries with a man torn between the contentment of family life and the pursuit of ambition and adventure as a single man.

ISBN 978-0-7531-9426-3 (hb)
ISBN 978-0-7531-9427-0 (pb)